THE MASK OF LOVE

Kennikat Press
National University Publications
Multi-disciplinary Studies in the Law

Advisory Editor
Honorable Rudolph J. Gerber

THE MASK OF LOVE
CORRECTIONS IN AMERICA
Toward A Mutual Aid Alternative

DENNIS SULLIVAN

Foreword by LARRY TIFFT

National University Publications
KENNIKAT PRESS // 1980
Port Washington, N.Y. // London

Manufactured in the United States of America

Published by
Kennikat Press Corp.
Port Washington, N.Y. / London

Library of Congress Cataloging in Publication Data

Sullivan, Dennis C
    The mask of love.

    (Multi-disciplinary studies in law) (National
university publications)
    Bibliography: p.
    Includes index.
    1. Corrections—United States. 2. Rehabilitation
of criminals—United States. 3. Community-based
corrections—United States. I. Title.
HV9304.S84   364.6'0973   79-22450
ISBN 0-8046-9256-4

I dedicate this work to

Hans Mattick ◊ *Leslie Wilkins* ◊ *John Sullivan*

and to all those whose true song remains, through our blindness to the essence of being human, unsung, unknown, or unwritten. I consider it a privilege to know or have known the true songs of these individuals.

CONTENTS

PART THREE: (*continued*)

THE MASK OF LOVE

PREFACE

Each of us, when confronted with instances where we have compromised ourselves, comes face to face with what I call admissions of self. These admissions of self are essentially a process where we recognize a compromised situation, one where we have been treasonous to ourselves, to the possibility of growing up some more, of becoming more whole, more sane, freer. Because these admissions counteract the conceptions we had lived by till then, those structures which had served us to the point of compromise, these admissions come hard. They bring pain and suffering. We are faced with more of the darkness of our existence, new fears, new impulses, the material of self we had not considered previously.

Oddly enough, without these confrontations with self we become immobile and sedentary. We grow like bulbous carrots deformed in rocky soil. After a while we begin to decay. But with them we gain insight, a new sense of direction, increased awareness. In a somewhat magical way a path is charted for us to follow. Resources and tools emerge that enable us to move along sanely amidst the pursuing complexity of life. We go along until we reach the next dead end, the next point of compromise, another choice to make regarding our future. The process of both personal and social evolution goes this way. Even Darwinists would agree.

In speaking of the journey poets take to grow or become more whole, to get in touch with the inspiration that enables them to experience, the poet Marvin Bell says: "Sometimes I think a poet's growth can be charted partly in terms of his or her becoming less and less embarrassed about more and more." This is an accurate description of the process of admissions of self described above. Perhaps the process applies to poets in a special way, but it is not one that is theirs exclusively. It is real for each

1

and every one of us. We all progress or fail according to how we face and resolve these admissions of self.

I also believe that the same is true for cultures, for groups and tribes, for whole civilizations. In the same way as individuals, whole civilizations are faced with admissions of self. These are collective admissions about their own forms of treason, their own forms of failure and compromise, which history tells us over and over are the failure to share responsibility for what happens to each of their members, particularly when the freedom of individuals is distorted or twisted in some way.

The history of evolution demonstrates that civilizations organize themselves in ways to produce their own internal energies to survive their failures or treasons. They give birth to people and artifacts who cleanse, who teach, who convince—in short, who do what is necessary to give us a chance. That's it, to give us a chance. Perhaps the ultimate criterion for assessing any work of art or sociology or physics or any human act is whether it gives us a chance, a chance to survive both as individuals and as a community. Any work that professes to be human must contain this latter element of collectivity, some sense of shared responsibility for life or mutual aid. I often wonder what occurred among the Maya so that they disappeared as a civilization, in what way they refused or denied the necessary admissions of self. There is a correlation to be taken into account in this matter of social evolution, a direct correlation; it is that between the extent, intensity, and nature of admissions of shared responsibility for life and the degree to which each is given a chance to survive, to achieve some modicum of well being.

Today America, the entire world, suffers from not giving itself a chance. Human trust has become as rare a quality as political honesty, mutual aid as rare as corporate compassion. This is the essence of our crime problem. As a country, as a world community, we have denied the responsibility we have for each other's needs and well being. We have denied the element of shared responsibility for life. We have refused to see that personal well being is related to shared economic responsibility. We refuse to pierce through the mask that conceals the relationship that exists between power economics and human enslavement, between the state's power to imprison and our own addiction to being controlled by that state. We are a culture swelling with the need for admissions of self, but they do not come. I believe it is because we have become too ashamed of ourselves and too fearful of what the shame, owned up to, might bring.

Americans today speak less and less of freedom. The word approaches the status of an archaism in our language. Twenty years ago the word was more a part of people's vocabulary; but that was the freedom of imperialism, of corporate economic interests—essentially human enslavement. I would postulate that we no longer talk of freedom because we have no maps to chart a way to that kind of someplace else. Those that promise conquest are useless for we realize that when we batter the head of another, we batter our own. The only possibility we have for freedom now is that based on mutual aid, interdependence and world harmony. But the maps for this possibility will not be forthcoming until each of us begins to make the necessary admissions of self, to admit that we are part of one worldwide community, that when people starve elsewhere each of us starves in some way, that when we sell arms to any nation or refuse food or fuel we prepare our collective holocaust.

Often admissions of self fail to come because we do not understand. We find ourselves ignorant and confused about what to say. We desire to speak, but what to say we see as a mystery. So we say we have no words to name the darkness, and avoid our task. In the present work I have attempted to put names on some of the confusion I see about why we hurt each other, about the ways we use to correct ourselves for the supposed well being of each of us. I have attempted to walk through some of the darkness that enshrouds us as a community and leaves us exiles in our own universe. I have attempted to call attention to and name the confusion where I saw it and was not afraid to approach it. I have attempted to provide a context in which each of us can begin to think about the choice for freedom within community.

You who do not agree that our human problems are collective, or as I see them, I urge to begin to express yourselves from the point of your own disagreement with and confusion about what I have proposed. I urge you to carve out a vision for yourselves, with your own personal imprint and experience, using your own confusion and frustration as a starting point. If you too find no sympathetic or understanding listeners to what you have uncovered, at least you will have unmasked for yourselves some of your own confusion about what is humanly possible. You will not have forfeited your own identities or been treasonous to yourselves in your own work. You will have charted for yourselves a new direction, new maps, with new awareness about self, about community, about the struggle to be human. There will be more hope for quality of life for everyone in the universe, for one more will have struggled for all. I acknowledge here those who have already done so and inspired me to begin and complete this work, in particular Ivan Illich, Gabriel Moran, Lewis Mumford and Wendell Berry. Their continued influence on my thinking is evident throughout this work.

Books on crime and punishment, criminal justice, and corrections are generally descriptive in nature, technical, banal, and narcissistic supports of the culture and structure of a social order. This book is a radical, analytical, restorative departure from what has gone before. It is radical in that it bares our roots, ideas, and sentiments and plants them in the human soil of feeling, thought, and interaction, as well as in the natural soil of the universe. It is analytical in its critical, reflective, and yet transcendent understanding of both existential and collective life. It is restorative in that it attempts to understand harms and power in relation to human experience and to unmask the tools which best facilitate the potential of humankind.

The metamorphizing power of this book is that it links corrections or "tools designed for safety" with the quality of our life. To understand the development of corrections we must understand that corrections as now practiced is a mask of love, an institutional concealment of our true selves and resources which prevents our living peacefully with one another. An understanding of the presence and nature of such a mask can be perceived only through an analysis of economics, power, social stratification, statecraft, the construction of meaning, and the professional control of human needs.

Piercing such a mask reveals the possible—that we can live in solidarity, that through mutual aid we can create and restore honest relationships with one another which do not require masks. To unmask corrections unveils the fact that the tools presently in use in our culture are counterproductive to personal and social unity and thus mutual trust and safety. In demystifying corrections we can explore the debilitating psychological and relational effects of the mode of production and the hierarchical power arrangements in our society, the conditions which form an institutional shackle on our collective soul. We can discover how corrections is reflective of the engineered tools which menace the survival of humankind, threaten the physical structure of the universe, undermine our participation in useful activity, deaden our creative imagination, threaten our diversity, and usurp our autonomy.

The current way of thinking about crime and corrections, the current set of questions — What causes crime? Who commits crimes? Does punishment deter? Is rehabilitation effective?—affirm the belief that safety is not an economic, political, or structural issue but rather one of personal or group pathology. It is through analysis of this mask that we see how and why crime and punishment are presented as distinct, separate behavioral entities. And it is through an analysis of this mask that the necessity of exploring alternative conceptions of person, social order, and justice is revealed. For example, in settings wherein mutual aid and caring relationships predominate, the feelings of commiseration, equality, and solidarity encourage the development of the principle of justice—to each according to his or her needs, within the resources available to the community. Justice based on need replaces the rights- and merit-based conceptions of current society.

The presentation of crime and punishment as discrete behavioral entities serves to exempt the powerful from incrimination for their harms and to cloak the fact that penal sanctions as well as crimes are intended harms. The violent, punishing acts of the state and its controlling professions are of the same genre as the violent acts of individuals. In each instance these acts reflect an attempt to monopolize human interaction, to control another person as if he or she were a commodity. This mask is not, however, a recent creation, for historically the aim of penal sanctions and its controlling masks has been the protection of those few able to define themselves beyond incrimination, and the sanctification of hierarchy. As Rusche and Kirchheimer have documented, punishments correspond to the current system of production and statecraft. The mode of punishment and the shape and expression of each mask heralded by the state has been dependent on historically and geographically specific economic and social conditions.

Corrections thus reflects the character of our present materialistic society. It reflects a transfer of responsibility, an atrophy of personal and collective autonomy and competence. As Illich has shown, our society has become one in which professionally engineered commodities have succeeded in replacing culturally shaped use values. The use value of our feet is given up for time-consuming, energy-intensive movement. The use value of our minds, of our curiosity, feeling, contemplation, and creativity is given up for stupefying educational instruction. As commodities have multiplied, we have developed an incapacity to grow food, sing, build, and care for one another. Rendered impotent to shape and to satisfy our needs, we are dependent on professions to diagnose needs and prescribe commodities. In deadening the will for independent experience, coerced education transforms learning from an activity we undertake to something we obtain. Caring for others becomes something we purchase rather than a practice and concern we share. And yet purchased professional health care is a nemesis which creates sickness, reinforces an industrial megamachine that generates ill health, undermines our competence in growing up and aging, and makes synthetic our struggle with pain and anguish. Human experience is thrust into the culture of ownership, appropriation, and consumption.

Dependence on the state for personal and social safety is the culmination of our cultural dependency on the disabling professions. Corrections professionals assert that only they can produce safety in the community. They insist that both persons and communities are incapable of self-reliance and autonomy. In their view, we are incapable of living together peacefully; indeed, we are the very reason for the need of corrections.

When we accept dependency on their professional prescription, the presence of social harms and personal conflicts is not viewed as a human condition necessary for creative assessment, change, or the development of new consciousness. Instances of harm and conflict are not viewed as opportunities to evaluate ourselves, to consider the needs of others, or to satisfy any needs in a personal manner. There is no conception of collective responsibility, but rather, requests for more police, more prisons, more coercive therapy, and a state-administered welfare economy. Instead of accepting responsibility for ourselves and each other, instead of directly settling our conflicts and disputes, we demand the state's social anesthesia.

Yet we know that love, compassion, sensitivity, justice, and equality, the basic elements of a "safe" society, can not be purchased. They are not commodities, nor are we. These relationships require a daily foundation in mutual aid and shared responsibility for each other, not exploitation, hierarchy, and external correction. It is thus that the primary function of present-day corrections is not to foster human experience or bonding but rather to.contain, monitor and consume. It is, as Michel Foucault has pointed out, to discipline and incapacitate. Corrections is now the state's master commodity; its mandarins, the master professionals.

These new mandarins do not search for truth, justice, or reconstruction of our society. They search for maximum deterrence with maximum legitimacy, efficacy in policies involving divestment, flat or presumptive sentencing, and welfare, and the maximization of discipline, obedience, and incapacitation to the point of forestalling serious threat of revolt. Person and community become institutional wards.

To understand the correctional complex is to understand what is the mask of love, a substitute for direct face-to-face living together. As Goodman makes clear, "safety" can emerge only when we are neither resigned nor fatalistic. It is a possibility only when we take ourselves and others seriously, when we take risks, develop our diverse talents to do useful work, and feel linked in real community. As long as we demand more consumables, we can not heap criticism on professionals. Rather, we must recognize that we create our tools, our relationships, our structures, and our masks; and therefore we are responsible for establishing community and shedding the mask of corrections.

As more of us are absorbed by corrections, by the state's disabling professions, more will experience the treadmill of consumption and thus seek more intimate affective ties than are now structurally possible. As these relations are formed, more persons will experience and learn that solidarity and affective feeling can not be satisfied through hierarchy and possession. Interacting with others as equals leads to sharing goods according to need, respecting the dignity of each person, and having equal access to resources owned by no one. Such experiences and feelings foster and are fostered by structural conditions wherein stratification and hierarchy are situational and temporary, wherein the division of labor is symbiotic and autonomous, wherein there is personal and interpersonal stability and yet constant risk and change, and wherein persons are recognized as unique and yet similar. It is toward these constructed relations that one finds in this book a personal shedding of masks and a sharing of new human vistas.

I

THE NATURE OF CORRECTIONS

imagine there's no heaven
it's easy if you try
no hell below us
above us only sky
imagine all the people
living for today . . .

imagine there's no countries
it isn't hard to do
nothing to kill or die for
and no religion too
imagine all the people
living life in peace . . .

imagine no possessions
i wonder if you can
no need for greed or hunger
a brotherhood of man
imagine all the people
sharing all the world . . .

you may say i'm a dreamer
but i'm not the only one
i hope someday you'll join us
and the world will be as one

John Lennon

1

A STARTING POINT

Corrections As Commodity

Twenty years ago the word "corrections" as a term that contained meaning in itself was not a part of our language. The emergence of the word as a self-contained entity is highly significant to those concerned about issues of crime, punishment, and justice, for its presence requires a radically different framework for posing questions about these matters. The term does not reflect simply the enormous growth in personnel and hardware that is taking place in the American correctional system or the updating and broadening in scope of an antiquated, nineteenth-century penology, as most professionals surmise. Rather, I believe that "corrections" is a term of despair and breakdown, stemming from a quantum leap into centralized existence. It reflects a new way we have come to relate to each other for our safety. It reflects an economy of relationship that regards the processes, activities, feelings, and experiences that lead to community safety and social unity as a commodity that is defined, prepared, and delivered by a core of experts and consumed by a docile clientele.

This economy of relationship—whether in a capitalist or state socialist context—is based on the belief that outside the state-professional complex there is no salvation, no personal rehabilitation, healing, or growth, no community integration or safety. Those who believe that this situation constitutes a severe crisis for human beings are faced with an additional dilemma, since within the social conditions prescribed by this twentieth-century multinational existence, as Ivan Illich notes, "crisis has come to mean that moment when doctors, diplomats, bankers, and assorted social engineers take over and liberties are suspended" (1978:4), not when people huddle together to provide for each other through mutual aid.

While this commodity orientation with respect to safety may be new, it is not an entirely new phenomenon or for that matter one that is singular to corrections and justice. It is rather part of a larger cultural illusion that we are born consumers and that we can attain happiness, freedom, social progress only through the purchase of goods and services from experts and certifying professions—namely, the state and now even enterprising individuals who set themselves up in their homes as alternative service-delivery units, reimbursed by public agencies or health insurance corporations for helping their neighbors. It is my contention that within such a framework corrections, both as a concept and as a massive industrial complex, has emerged and has come to assume the social significance we give to professionalized medicine, education, and perhaps even religion.

For those who fear we approach a police state daily, I believe that the movement and nature of correctional activity is a good barometer. While a few years ago many working in the correctional complex clamored that everything was becoming "police-ized," a slight variation on this theme seems to be coming true—that is, all the personnel of the state justice system, the courts, and even the police themselves are becoming "correctionalized." If there is immanent danger of a police state, it is not simply in therapists or helpers of the justice system carrying guns and making arrests, but in all state-professional functionaries, including police, adjusting people on the street with newly learned therapeutic techniques. This has the effect of turning the last remnant of the communal village, the autonomous neighborhood, into a ward.

As I mentioned, the change that has occurred in corrections is not a singular phenomenon but can be understood in relation to all human services. The same commodity orientation can be found in medicine, education, work, and religion, where basic human needs and their satisfaction are treated as a commodity to be purchased as a service produced or performed by someone else—namely, the expert. A person purchases sanity from a therapist, earns an education from a teacher, regains health from a physician, alleviates fears of being hurt from a public safety specialist, and is reborn by receiving revelation from a mediary. These terms and concepts put human experience into a world of ownership, production, and consumption. They are part of the character of our present market-intensive society in which convivial or social means toward community are being replaced by what Illich refers to as "manipulative industrial ware" (1978:3).

For some people such a framework might be seen as an indirect incrimination of what they do, for it places the agencies and agents of justice as well as the total complex of human services squarely in the political-economic arena, a context in which those involved in help delivery have struggled not to see themselves. It is seen as an affront to the helping image. But it is precisely within this framework of need satisfaction as political economy that corrections has emerged and receives its meaning. Whether corrections is viewed as a means to correct crime, issue punishment, or generate safety in communities, it reflects a professionalized commodity orientation toward human experience. It is the opposite of mutual aid, a social, face-to-face process of which each of us is capable.

A necessary concomitant of this growing commodity orientation toward human experience has been the disappearance or growing in-inaccessibility, perhaps even the permanent loss, of the resources tools, or instincts of mutual aid—the instincts of sociality by which we foster a face-to-face existence. The concept and practice of mutual aid that once bonded people together as neighbors has been nearly totally displaced by professionalism, self-reliance by law, neighborliness by commodities and services, the sharing of gifts and hospitality by payment and insurance plans.

As our social relationships become increasingly those of strangers, unwilling or unable to provide safety or protection for each other freely by mutual aid, we find ourselves collectively coming full circle—that is, we find ourselves having to purchase mutual aid as a commodity individually. It should come as no surprise that there are increasing numbers of people, whom I refer to as "correctionalists," who make a living off the effects of these stranger relationships, of the forfeiture of mutual aid, in the same way that educators live on society's alienation from self, doctors prosper on the division between work and leisure that has destroyed health, and politicians thrive on the distribution of welfare which, in the first instance, was financed by those they are paid to assist. Illich has described how these institutions have become forms of appropriation and erode our sense of competency and autonomy (1978:4). While in the narrow sense the term "correctionalist" may refer to a criminologist, a criminal justice bureaucrat, a policymaker, a researcher, a planner, or any person who delivers or produces justice as a commodity, the term extends to anyone who teaches or heals or consoles another through the circuitous route of commodity and paid service.

Whereas once dependence on commodities or purchase for survival was a sign of bad times—the gravity of one's hardship assessed by how much a person had to purchase from another for survival—in our present culture consumption and purchase have become a sign of personal worth, something to be counted as a blessing and shown off. To *have* a therapist, a lawyer, a string of personal physician-specialists for every part of the body, or to have had a certified education is considered a sign of prosperity. The same applies to correcting our hurts or social harms. To *have* a well-managed, well-financed, professionally staffed, well-researched justice complex that produces safety is considered a sign of progress. This purchase orientation must be understood in a still larger social-economic context, that of having needs or being needy in our present society. To be without, to be needy, is among the greatest social disgraces. Ironically, it has become less a disgrace to purchase one's needs or necessities from a professional stranger—even if it entails becoming a captive to the supplier—than to admit one's dependence and seek support for it from one's neighbors. The result is that there always remain hidden away one's needs, frailty, emptiness, loneliness, those elements that give each of us personal definition (our uniqueness) and bring us together to support each other through mutual aid.

Clearly, this consumptive way of life, while resolving individual status and social control needs, is counterproductive to mutual support and cooperation in the human struggle. As individuals go from office to office, service to service, purchase to purchase for personal meaning, the continuity of self, of relationship, of community, that once signified human bonding and prosperity for the species dwindles and soon disappears. Life does not entail the pursuit of a lifework or the development of community, for these are not considered personal matters or matters of personal journey where one moves along continually asking, why do I exist? Rather, life becomes a series of packages to be consumed, purchases to be made for which one makes appointments and by which one schedules one's entire life. The whole notion of freedom has been wiped from the human landscape.

In our present culture the avoidance of self-reliance and mutually supportive relationships on a face-to-face basis is so great that we have become a paralyzed culture, helpless as persons and communities. Human exchange is now by way of violence, greed and exploitation. One measure of the gravity of the paralysis is the thousands upon thousands of self-help books written each year informing the public how to survive within their privatized, commodity-based worlds. Like the pills they often replace, they are in effect temporary tools for surviving current social-economic imprisonment. It is not possible to denigrate the value of these books totally, for through the techniques and skills outlined in them many people are capable of making some sense of their own value in a devalued multinational world. However, as far as social evolution goes, as far as community-based autonomy goes, they lead the species (by what they omit) into, so it seems, irretraceable cul-de-sacs. The notions of mutual aid, interdependence, and community are treated as factors extraneous to the particular malaise one has contracted or thinks one has contracted.

If the problem of personal and community paralysis is as pervasive a phenomenon as I have stated, why concentrate on corrections, seemingly a more narrow and often ill-defined area of study? Why intertwine matters of corrections and justice with those of mutual aid? To answer the latter question first, I believe that all significant matters of correcting severed relationships, whether these be referred to as corrections, penology, therapy, or confession, have their foundation in mutual aid, in shared responsibility for each other's needs. If any system of correcting or justice is to be human and equitable, it cannot be through institutions such as prisons or through social principles such as power and punishment. Human and equitable treatment comes only through face-to-face relationship in communities bonded by mutual aid. The concentration on corrections is a good starting point for understanding human relationship. By focusing on the principles and tools of punishment, we can begin to understand the most prevalent way we have chosen to relate to each other in the twentieth century.

Second, I am focusing on corrections because my own professional history is there. A treatise of this nature is necessarily autobiographical. To a large extent this book represents my continued movement away from a professional career in corrections and criminal justice, toward establishing a more human foundation of justice based in mutual aid. The administrative context of justice promoted in professional schools in this country I have found to be too narrow and too punishing for those who ask the kinds of questions I find personally important. In my own attempts to foster solidarity, create community, live justly and freely in these institutions, chairmen, deans, and administrators have called my attention to the lack of value in such work because of its lack of professionalism and career-relatedness. I am simply reminded of Paul Goodman: "Insistently and consistently applied, any human value, such as common sense, honor, honesty, or compassion, will soon take one far out of sight of the world as it is, and to have meaning is one of the virtues that is totally disruptive of established institutions" (1977b:283).

Finally, I have come to know in the search for meaning in my work many people involved in the administration of justice as professionals who are extraordinary human beings, with extraordinary human potential, but whom I have found confused by bureaucratic exchanges and by the vicious-circle ideologies in which professional justice issues are presently ensconced. Many are no longer capable of living by the principles of law. Punishment as a way to correct human hurts makes no sense to them. Many, having come to accept personal revolution as inevitable in their own lives, find emerging theories of crime and justice too impersonal and possessive of what is human; the ideology takes precedence over experience, and the spontaneous, feeling components of ourselves, so long in exile, are guarded and contained by the state with the same degree of apprehension as they are within capitalist institutions. The new realism theories that regard punishment and power as the means toward social bonding are seen as too frightening in the way they casually minimalize life, and the remnants of liberal ideologies are seen as transparently shallow and meaningless for understanding community, for they deny the significance of political economy in understanding the well being, growth, and healing of the human spirit. These displaced people are all in a very real sense exiles, for they see all ideologies that have a starting point beyond the human as harmful to experience. If I were pressed to pinpoint an audience for this book, it would be these exiles for whom now the only alternative seems to be a career of quiet despair, as well as those who are being recruited into these professional positions only to have a similar life experience.

2

MUTUAL AID

A Context for Choice

The introduction of mutual aid as a context for understanding corrections, justice, or safety is for many people an anomaly. Mutual aid has not been a part of the professional sociological or criminological tradition, or for that matter part of the political tradition in which corrections and justice are presently rooted. An exploration of the history of corrections, penology, and penal sanction, by way of documents, books, artifacts, and the neighborhood traditions of people, reveals rather quickly that its contents are entirely a description of the ways and means by which bureaucracy, the state, and the richer classes regulate and enslave people and communities. The substance of correctional history in particular is in fact the struggles among economic-political elites, forces external to community, a log of their acts to survive and maintain their establishment among the endless attempts by people to create community safety through self-reliance and mutual aid. Our present history supports what Kropotkin wrote nearly a hundred years ago: "The mutual-aid factor has been hitherto totally lost sight of; it was simply denied, or even scoffed at, by the writers of the present and past generation" (1902:45). The same sentiments are applicable today, for mutual aid is part of an entire tradition that has been discarded, overlooked, hidden because of its political-economic consequences. Few students of justice today realize that years before Marx and Engels wrote the *Communist Manifesto* Proudhon had already emerged as the protagonist of an economic interpretation of history, with mutual aid as a foundation for experience and community (Woodcock, 78–79).

The irony is that when the state and its certifying professions found it advantageous to take the community as its locus for treatment of crime, insanity, and ignorance (to compete, I maintain, with the efforts of those who pushed for community-based competencies), the state and its institutions became increasingly vulnerable to being assessed and judged not solely by political expediency standards but by those principles that historically were proved to keep communities bound together and safe— namely, mutual aid. Using the relational standards of mutual aid as a measuring rod rather than political expediency, one becomes quickly aware that the state is not "the master of the world, the author of the only universally valid culture, the center of the only real and useful science, and so on" (Eliade, 51). One discovers rather quickly that the state is a tool or composite of resources, *not* superior to individuals but in fact containing and fostering the very elements (organizationally and politically) that it points to as innately dangerous defects in individuals (genetically and psychologically) and in autonomous communities. It is asserted that the bureaucratic qualities which the state cultivates to control and isolate individuals are basic, human qualities. Attempts are made to mask this distinction by making the assumption that what is good for the growth of the system is also good for individuals. Erich Fromm notes:

This construction was bolstered by an auxiliary construction that the very qualities that the system required of human beings—egotism, selfishness, and greed—were innate in human nature; hence, not only the system but human nature itself fostered them. . . .People refused to recognize that these traits were not natural drives that caused industrial society to exist, but that they were the *products* of social circumstances. [7-8]

Seen from the framework of mutual aid, the state and its claims about creating sociality or safe social conditions become highly transparent. There is a fresh opportunity to look at the role of the state and the professional complex as a corrector of crime, as the provider of safety. We begin to see that despite the endless contentions of correctionalists, through a changing array of philosophies, theories, and program inventions, the American correctional complex has never had a positive influence in correcting people, in helping them or making them whole. Nor can it! The very term "correctional" is a misnomer and more—it is a mask, a mask of love.

If anyone can point to any growth on the part of people as individuals or solidarity within the neighborhoods or communities in America, it is due to mutual aid, to the shared experiences or cooperative efforts of people struggling together outside the domain of the state system, as Lewis Mumford characterizes it, the efforts of people "nibbling at the edges of the power structure" (1970:408). While it might have been possible for correctionalists to have disputed such a contention years ago by citing institutionalized measures such as recidivism rates and what correctionalists refer to as hard scientific data, even these traditional system supports belie state-professional competency. The soulless nature of the correctional complex, its language, the way people are directed and ordered about, the continual procession of theories and philosophical justifications for punishment that come and go like clothing fashions, disqualify the system from any human or unifying experience. Compassion, justice, freedom, the basic elements of a safe society, have been a real impossibility for those who work within the political-economic confines of the correctional system. Freedom, justice, compassion require a foundation of mutual aid, not power, hierarchy, and estrangement.

Corrections is a business, a corporate enterprise that markets the mask of love as a substitute for love. It is a grand complex of agencies in the form of probation, parole, jails, halfway houses, group homes, diversion programs, and now a seemingly infinite number of administrative variations on these themes. At the center of this complex stands the American penitentiary, its cherished centerpiece and the continuing source of definition for all its satellite activities, right down to the progressive group home.

The primary function of this enterprise is not to foster human experience or bonding in communities but to contain, to monitor, those who live within as well as outside the rules of the state. Within the prison correctionalists do this primarily through the deprivation of light, sound, touch, and breath. Outside the prison their punishing activities also have the effect of disabling people. They discredit the inner resources of people to provide for themselves, denying to people their own struggle for communal safety. Moreover, the centralized, hierarchical correctional system with its prison—the epitome of competitive, centralized existence—serves as an ongoing model for those who seek a totalitarian society, a total commodity-based existence. The system is a social context in which every human need is treated as a commodity—defined, supplied, and satisfied by the state—each person treated as a ward of the state, all mutually supportive communication regarded as defiance to state administrative control. Even the usual activities of reform, change, and innovation are geared not toward fostering cooperation and mutual support among people but toward totalizing life; they are attempts, as Illich notes, to "systematically expropriate environmental conditions that foster individual and group autonomy" (1978:16).

In coming to grips with the somewhat intense meaning of these statements, one begins to grasp a second major function of the American correctional system, the creation and propagation of myths about the competency of the state and its core of professional experts to correct relationship. Correctionalists assert in both theory and practice that only their professional, scientifically based, problem-solving methods (rehabilitation, just deserts, capital punishment) can produce safety in community. They harp upon the innate inability of the human person and communities to be self-reliant and autonomous, to live peacefully through mutual aid. They insist that the power to correct must reside in the state and professional experts, or else communities will break down into even more paralyzing chaos. Only state officialdom has the expertise and resources to understand industrialized relationship properly and thereby provide for the safety, sanity, and health of people through its certifying institutions and professions. In theory and practice correctionalists attempt to convince people that their bodies, skills, feelings are useless for bonding themselves together—indeed, that the presence of these human qualities is the very reason for the need of the state certification. In a very real sense state correctional activities are a form of societal self-indulgence, *for they have nothing to do with the renewal of social connections that provide a context for the well being of each person.*

The ideology of the state and its professions rules out the possibility that the correction of crime, the development of human safety, is an activity related to the basic struggle of every human being to take charge of his or her own fate in the context of a community of mutual support. From the state-professional point of view, to believe otherwise is to approach the realm of treason; to behave otherwise is to enter it! As I hope to demonstrate, the "cure" that the state-professional complex forces upon us only serves to perpetuate the dread disease of alienation.

If community health or safety is the result of people struggling cooperatively and providing for each other's well being freely, that is, through mutual aid, correctionalists are now among the most significant factors in inhibiting the development of safe, autonomous communities. Their own continuation and growth as provider of safety services is dependent upon the continuing demise and disintegration of the habit or instinct of mutual aid. In fact, the person, the group, the neighborhood that is autonomous, self-directing, and self-reliant becomes a natural enemy to the correctionalist and the state, for its presence denies dependence upon and need for state-professional commodities. In a variation of the survival of the fittest theme, correctionalists compete with the autonomous neighborhood for establishing a sense of reality.

One does not have to reach too far to conclude that the American correctional system is one of the major deterrents to solving what Americans have come to refer to as the crime problem, for it detracts from the very processes that encourage people to take charge of their own lives and to develop the commitment to each other that disallows social harms and violence. In effect, those who support the activities of the American correctional system (corrections as profession and commodity) support the continuation and growth of violence and social integration in America. They relegate to a position of vestigial organ or historical artifact the processes that reduce our being strangers to each other, that restore connectedness with the universe we live in. In many ways the crime problem is a societal version of the so-called identity crisis. The latter is a result of the disconnection of body and soul (opening up a new industry of therapist professionals), while the crime problem is the result of the disconnection of body from earth, opening up a new industry of control professionals in the form of the corrections-industrial complex. While both reflect kinds of harm that need to be taken seriously, both the identity crisis and crime problem are a profitable genre of self- and societal indulgence. As Wendell Berry comments on the identity crisis: "It can be an excuse for irresponsibility or a fashionable mode of self-dramatization. It is the easiest form of self-flattery—a way to construe procrastination as a virtue—based on the romantic assumption that 'who I really am' is better in some fundamental way than the available evidence proves" (111).

I am beginning with the premise that there can be no reduction in violence, no movement toward community and social intimacy, no resolution of the politically based crime problem, as long as people forfeit their own resources or tools for intimacy to the state and its professions, a monopoly of which these latter require for their continued credibility and survival. Similarly, I am beginning with the premise that community solidarity can occur only through a subsistence economy, an economy of connectedness with the universe, in which people make what they use by means of traditional tools, in which they heal what they hurt in mutual aid, face-to-face relationships.

In short, I am asserting that the primary locus of personal and social unity—whether we call it healing, correcting, learning, or justice—cannot be found in any standardizing system or style of management but is rooted in the human viscera and the cooperation of people toward the well being of each person. Justice is a principle, as Proudhon asserted,

. . . secreted within him, it is immanent. It constitutes his essence, the essence of society itself. It is the true form of the human spirit, a form which takes shape and grows toward perfection only by the relationship that every day gives birth to social life. Justice, in other words, exists in us like love, like notions of beauty, of utility, of truth, like all our powers and faculties. Justice is human, completely human, nothing but human. . . .
[1858]

Our present sense of how to live together seems to contradict such a sentiment, for we have become prisoners to a system of production that supports notions of self and relationship that are personally disabling, away from mutual aid. As a society we now believe that an enriched form of slavery is preferable to the everyday struggle to live freely with others. Self-determination is equated with institutional regulation exemplified by the current wave of "meism" that Wolfe (1976) and Lasch (1979) see as permeating our culture. That the human person is or can be trusted, can be responsive to others, can be a self-regulating actor in his or her own growth and maturity is no longer accepted as part of current institutional reality. It is not surprising that we live in a society most regard as unsafe, rather than one in which people are trusted to aid each other and meet each other's needs. Only through mutual aid, as we will see later, can people be bound to each other so they feel connected and safe.

If we can begin with any accord about what we refer to as harmony or safety, it is that there can be no harmony or safety with self and with others within a system that expropriates this self and community for its own maintenance. This latter being the case in our present society, it is up to each individual to make a choice: either to opt for self-determination and autonomous community or to remain within the tutelage of the state-professional complex. It is a paradox of the highest degree: if we wish to correct our crime problems and unify society, make it safe for all of us, if we wish to be a free and human society in which the well being of each is a real concern, we must scrap and build around the very organizational complex that has been set up by the state to do these very things. The first step is to begin to question the value of the state system and the professional in our lives to whose endless list of prescription slips we seem to have become addicted.

3

CORRECTIONAL ASSUMPTIONS

What Is Central?

The statements above are not intended as an attempt to inject sensationalism or overstatement into a fumbling and confused body of theory so as to draw the crowds into a new correctional side show. If we lack an understanding of human community and safety, especially as they relate to corrections and justice, it is because corrections has been deluged with a plethora of side shows, act after act coated with political rhetoric or moral salvation statements that serve only to protect the status quo. In consonance with the current era of industrial management packages, correctionalists now cloak these acts in the language of "change strategies" which, translated, means the expert distribution of commodities and the tightening of the professional fist around the consumer's competence to do things for himself. The packaging that occurs is itself a sign of social distance among people. As Paul Goodman states, "When the consumption of a product is far removed from its production—removed by the geographical distance between factory and home, removed by the economic distance of sale and resale up to the retail, and removed by the temporal distance between making and use—the product is encased in a series of Packages" (1977c:51). The irony is that professionally based change strategies, however enticing the wrapping of their packages, have provided a false sense of hope for people. They always prove to be geared not toward the development of self-reliant persons and community-based competencies but toward shoring up a failing state apparatus and bureaucratic procedure that suffer continually from administrative lag.

Nor am I attempting subtly to issue another in the growing history of abolish-everything statements, the beginning of a new brand of radical romanticism. To regain a sense of community and of what it means to be human it is not sufficient to smash capitalism or the state or simply to dismantle institutions and professions that disable. Brandishing hammers of political dismantling or smashing only serves to leave people tired and worn, with life experiences limited to destruction, dismantling, and their ideologies. This is one lesson we have learned from recent history, from the lives of people who spent themselves solely in protest and political revolution. Future-based revolutionary movements have only short-term shock value and provide little in the way of understanding our basic human needs and the conditions that foster sociality and human progress.

Rather, I hope to use our personal histories, our own personal struggles as a starting point for making sense of relationship for safety. If anything persists among those who have shown a professional or scientific interest in human transformation, particularly in the area of corrections, it is the thorough denial of their own personal histories as having any relevance for what they do in their work. Objectively, they superimpose new theory upon old theory, new program upon old program, newly created identity upon old-fashioned identities, all of which has the subtle but lasting effect of blending out the personal from life struggles, life struggles from political problem solving. So persistent are correctionalists to deliver *the* correct revelation, *the* way, that they lose all sense of their own needs for cooperating with all men and women to develop a meaning of community.

If we wish to bring about social unity, the social conditions that foster safety and justice, as Alex Berkman notes, "we must first learn to respect the humanity of ourselves, of each fellow human, neither invading nor coercing anyone; we must learn to consider each person's liberty as sacred as our own; to respect each person's freedom and personal style—to forswear compulsion in any form" (233). But if we examine the theoretical activities of correctionalists historically, we see that they have limited themselves mostly to battles of moral justifications or justifications for punishment, without any foundation in our bread-and-butter existence. It is not surprising that these justification battles often begin and end with sociological or moral abstractions expressed through such highly charged terms as "the just," "the wicked," and the like, for the central category is blame. The adoption of theories based on these kinds of abstractions entails no wrestling with one's convictions or any personal change, for that matter, only a change of mind, the differences wrestled with as negligible as that between justification by works and justification by faith in the late Reformation.

Perhaps what is most characteristic about current theories on crime, corrections, and justice is that they bracket out the economic-social foundations from which these abstract concepts are but ideological derivatives.

Change then is never a matter of personal assessment and risk for anyone, for it is not based on self-doubt. Consequently there is little or no new consciousness about personal and social reconstruction. Rather, change becomes a matter of enforcement and clashing wills, a matter of power to convince others of the most fashionable (a decade ago the term was "relevant") but absolute formulation of *the* correct world. An argument for grounding one's thinking in the basic everyday work and needs of people is put down as the idle talk of dreamers. "Why not do something practical?" is the common challenge, as if regrounding one's being in human relationship, in the universe, were not the most practical, the most straightforward way toward inner peace and social harmony.

With power, or battles of justification, as the means for gaining agreement on a sense of social reality, a means that encroaches on the most vulnerable parts of our humanity, it is not surprising that most people demonstrate an extraordinary defensiveness about and avoidance of personal involvement in their thinking about safety. Oddly enough, for many people writing about safety today, their safety as professionals, requires a bargaining position in which the possibility of mentioning anything about their own struggle to grow up is rejected. This results in the simultaneous rejection of what is human in others and therefore of the possibility of any alternate social-economic reality that has its roots in the human—for example, mutual aid. The core of the their lives consists of a kind of political infighting to protect a professional domain. The proverbial wars on crime and delinquency often boil down to a continuing war among professionals to maintain political domains for themselves, professional control over their ever-restless, ever-changing clienteles.

Many correctionalists find themselves in a bind, for by adhering to the political requirements of their professions they make it criminal or treasonous for themselves to entertain any alternate view of living together other than those based on the principles of power and competition. They say: "We have done our part through our organizational existence; ask no more of us." They succeed in turning "the modern state into a holding corporation of enterprises that facilitate the operation of their self-certified competencies" (Illich, 1978:23). And as available fiscal resources for maintaining legislatively prescribed clienteles fluctuate, the domain and ownership fights for wards of clientele are intensifying. New fashions in the mask of love are marketed, labeled "radical left" or "radical right" or "new realist," but these too have their foundations in state-professional competency, not in personal or community-based competencies that support the well being of every person. One result of these domestic fiscal changes, which have their roots in international economics (Tifft, 1979), has been the transformation of the traditional correctionalist into a new hybrid, the "statecrat," a civilian version of the regimented military automaton who survives by adhering to a strictly political definition of justice and life.

My concern in this book is with an inquiry into the assumptions upon which modern thinking about corrections rests, an inquiry into the philosophical foundations of punishment not in the narrow sense of correctional policy or correctional management, but in the more universal or pervasive sense of personal and social integration. In short, my concern is to give corrections a life context based not on the rights or merit of individuals but on the well being of each person. This entails from the outset a refusal to take the state or professional competency as our starting point. In searching for different ways toward social unity— different tools, different conceptions of life, self, and relationship— those elements or factors that impinge on our humanity so very directly, we can assume nothing.

To begin a treatise on corrections by raising questions about the centrality of the state and its certifying professions in our lives is an endeavor not endearing to most people, for the maintenance of their established lifestyles is dependent upon the avoidance of such questions. This is especially true for professional correctionalists who approach these questions "objectively," as if that were a real possibility. They justify their value-free lives through the requirements of scientific method, excluding any analysis of "soft and shaky positions." For these people, a discussion of corrections from a mutual aid context is to talk about life concepts that are not operational, not measurable, and therefore not real.

In addition, if one is a criminologist writing about justice issues without using the state as one's starting point, one is thought not to be writing authentic criminology. It is thought that one is not on the subject, as readers wait impatiently for the heart of the matter. For many people, the writing is actually thought to have a treasonous sound. To reject the state as the starting point, as happens in the Soviet Union when the state is decentralized conceptually, is tantamount to an open admission of the loss of one's sanity, a forfeiture of one's right to be free, for one has rejected the supposed source of truth.

If in fact there is an a priori, definable heart of the matter, I would suggest that we ought not to be too anxious to get to it. This is not a form of avoidance on my own part but an attempt to be open to a more realistic human perspective on safety. In this sense, the present work might be considered precorrectional in that its focus is the total situation of humankind, its conceptions of life, the world, and relationship.

For those who reject the possibility of a different kind of starting point I ask: suppose one neither accepts nor rejects the state-professional complex? Suppose one has an affinity for personal responsibility and autonomous community, finds the state-professional complex to be an inescapable element in our current life, approaches it with caution and intelligence, but is unable to suppose that it can be the center of one's life or life generally? By espousing such a position does one forfeit the place one already has in the human race? (Moran, 14–15).

There is an eagerness on the part of most people, particularly correctionalists, to avoid hearing these kinds of questions, to deny their validity on grounds of practicality. They would rather argue about the deterrence value of capital punishment or longer prison sentences or how prisons are disintegrating into country clubs. They simply put firm limits on what they will allow in their lives. More often than not the rationale is that it is the function of the state and its certifying professions to take care of these matters.

Duffee and Fitch, for example, in an introduction to a text on correctional policy, hurriedly provide a listing of underlying assumptions but dismiss a discussion of their present relevance: "We find entering the debate, let alone settling it, inconsequential to the present study and to solution of the pressing problems facing a society that is dependent on the current criminal justice system" (4). This avoidance may be the typical response to addressing correctional assumptions today but Duffee's statement is non-typical in that he admits that such questions exist and are relevant to a discussion of community-based competency for safety.

To avoid awareness of our assumptions about punishment and justice is to reduce life issues, whether they be issues of personal competence or cooperative living, to professional dilemmas, administrative and managerial exercises, data for policy design. Any discussion of the basic social conditions which contribute to human competence and human frailty is sidetracked. A system of norms for living together is created and enforced without any understanding of the foundations upon which those norms are based. Some of the most normative and enforcing people are totally unaware that they live by norms and that these norms require force for their preservation.

The irony in bypassing the issue of assumptions is that it is believed firmly that entering the debate about personal involvement in one's destiny is extraneous to life problems. With these kinds of limitations put on questions of living together, the correctionalist in effect gives the state correctional complex the good housekeeping seal, while in the meantime covers up and thereby threatens to destroy the very social and cultural resources needed by people to live a life of constant, autonomous corrections. A correctional framework, a view of justice, is set up in which experts expound upon a system, its policy and administration, without understanding the world and people for whom it exists.

Rarely, if ever, do modern correctionalists show a concern for discovering how and why our present society, or any culture for that matter, is so very dependent upon an impersonal system of control and regulation for its freedom, for correcting people who act impersonally. To question the impersonality requires the displacement of the conventional center of the professionals' lives, which for many individuals amounts to too great a personal risk. The result in our present society is the continuing relegation of safety to a commodity status, a social situation which, in its ultimate form, becomes the totalitarian state. The more immediate effect of settling for commodity as means is, as Slater argues, "to remove the underlying problems of our society farther and farther from daily experiences and daily consciousness and hence to decrease, in the mass of the population, the knowledge, skill, resources, and motivation necessary to deal with them" (15). We remove ourselves from the very materials that are the source or opportunities for personal growth, competence and freedom. If we are in fact a culture of fear-ridden people, the sociologist, criminologist, even the artist cannot continue to respond with greater doses of the medicine of expertise (blame and punishment). Expertise and professionalism, rather than fostering greater social interdependence, create greater distance among people and greater fears within people. Each person who is working for the community soon recognizes, as Paul Goodman asserts, that, "if persons are estranged from one another, from themselves, and from their artist, he takes the initiative precisely by putting his arms around them and drawing them together" (1977a:160).

The effects of such covering up of assumptions about life are evident everywhere. As a culture we have grown out of touch with ourselves; we see and feel ourselves to be powerless, without the resources to face in a direct way the human hurts that are part of the eternal struggle for meaning, that bond people together. We find many people living a form of schizo-existence in which personal responsibility for creating community is given over to the state in exchange for a share in the state's containment of human problems and in the ethically novocaining myth that mutual aid is not an essential aspect of creating safe, livable communities. Why, therefore, develop theories of social unity and freedom that derive from a locus of the human? It is this kind of thinking that has driven contemporary man and woman to see themselves as no longer a useful and necessary member of a social world, part of a meaningful plan of existence, within a cosmic or divine order, but as a superfluous, replaceable extension of a dying economic system. To play a variation on a theme of Nietzsche, if the state exists, humankind is superfluous. Yet, unless we come to grips with our own helplessness as alone, realizing that any significance we have is only in relation to the other, the ultimately real, including human misery, we will fail as humans. An essential part of freedom, safety, social harmony is an awareness of our connectedness with the other and a cooperation to maintain interdependence.

Why people avoid questioning the centrality of the state, why they insist on putting an upper limit to what they think about relationship, or to what they will allow themselves to say or do or feel outside the constructs of the state, is somewhat obscure to me. People set firm boundaries on what they will allow themselves to believe about crime, punishment, safety, human needs, hurts, even though their everyday experiences fly in the face of these beliefs. They argue for capital punishment and more professional management of others when all forms of punishment and management in their own lives—whether it be at work, in the hospital, at school, at church—narrow the human and creative possibilities they harbor within themselves. Some show a strange sort of nostalgia for relationship according to state prescriptions; a fear of sounding treasonous to their professional tradition or appearing deviant themselves prohibits them from any search for truth.

What is odd is that the people I am talking about admit that the state's ability to bring about a sense of community is myth, but for them to criticize an ailing system or institution when it is down seems wrong—even though the state might be a major force in their lives that brings them to despair. For them the state and professional ethics might be a fraud, politics might be crooked, the correctional system might be a political showcase, but "What else is there?" Denied the reality of the state and professional competency, they become immobilized over where to assign their loyalties next. Moreover, for many the system has meant work, a livelihood, security, something to hold on to, and deserves a certain amount of loyalty in return. Yet, by holding on to something that is personally meaningless, they reinforce their own dependence on a commodity existence, forfeiting the face-to-face involvement in life that brings about personal meaning and communities of human concern.

It is another irony that so many of the staunch defenders of the correctional complex ask to be shown what is better, to be given guarantees or proofs of living alternatives that might be more meaningful for their despairing selves. Solutions to living harmoniously are shopped for in the same way that packaged goods are, consumptively. Community safety is not thought of as the result of shared personal journeys, one that each person maps out for himself or herself and that unfolds as one goes about asking, Who am I? Does what I am doing have meaning for me? but as a reality imposed from without, through law, the state, professional prescriptions, which one consumes and lives by faithfully. Traditionally, when arguments have been made that reflect a new kind of starting point such as mutual aid, one that involves questioning one's religiously held assumptions about the state and capitalist economics, defensive postures are taken. One way to prevent new experiences from developing is to engage continually in apologies for what has been, what one *has*, to suppress any questioning of one's own present, internal reality. But sooner or later by living this way a person accedes to and becomes part of professional clientization, the fallout of an economic system unconcerned with the well being of each of us. I am arguing that it is no longer possible to live this way and disclaim one's own sharing in social harm. What may be needed most of all at a time like this is the courage to listen to and the courage to question what is not understood.

4

PRACTICAL CORRECTIONS

Certification and the Professional Life

The apathy and resistance we find among most social scientists toward examining their assumptions about relationship can be attributed in large part to the relationship they see between assumptions and theory. To many people—even those who refer to themselves as theorists—theory is seen as something intangible, as reflecting a movement away from solving immediate social problems. As Gouldner points out: "Theorizing is seen as a substitution of talking about problems rather than *doing* something about them. Social theory is viewed as a form of escapism, if not a form of moral cowardice" (27).

Among those who maintain or aspire to professional affiliations, there is an unequivocal insistence upon "the practical." We hear university students, faculty, bureaucrats, deans, journal editors, publishers and funding agencies insist upon the practical. Those with an economic interest in corrections single-mindedly express concern for "How practical is this program?" or "How down to earth is this teacher?" When examined more closely, these statements do not translate into: "Can we learn more about the basic principles for an ethical life's work?" or "Can we begin to understand the requirements of community that foster sociality?" but "Will this program or series of courses give me the necessary credentials for landing a job?" or "Will this grant proposal, if funded, produce better management techniques?" "The practical" becomes an idiom for the shortest route to job security, to selling publications, to controlling others, for it certifies a person to be a certifier. The practical gives an individual more facile entry into the political-economic arena. It is in many ways a professional club mentality that shuns any definition or source of help or aid that is not a delivered-consumed commodity.

The practical is a masked route for reducing everything to the realm of *problem,* which in turn sets the stage for professional intervention, intervention with expertise, for professional or scientific expertise is believed to produce experience or community by solving problems (e.g., the crime problem, the identity crisis). What Gabriel Marcel said of empiricism is true of this kind of professionalism; its fundamental error is "to take experience for granted and to ignore the mystery; whereas what is amazing and miraculous is that there should be experience at all."

The result of this concern for being certified is that critical life questions about human needs and well being, about imposed punishment as a means to healing and human growth, are explored only insofar as they fit within the framework of administrative needs, policy design constraints, outright job specifications, or tenure committee standards—the practical. If some semblance of theory or a social ideal is entertained, it is by way of providing justifications for punishment or state-professional intervention in our lives, addressed as reflecting the concerns of society at large—an abstraction! University curricula in particular have become pre–job training sessions, a particular brand of placement office counseling and licensing for professional practice. Grappling with present ethical and moral questions, with the nature of the professional tools being developed, is suppressed for more direct advancement within the profession.

Examining a university curriculum, therefore, one quickly has a sense that the study of corrections is much like preparation for being a plumber. It is as if 1 plus 1 always makes 2. There is no recognition of the fact that there is   seemingly limitless uncertainty to life, even mystery. A solid grounding in a professionalized "nuts and bolts"—the jargon, writing style, accepted theoretical boundaries, funding contacts—is thought to be an adequate preparation   for a life's work in justice! Most often the result is that the soon-to-be plumber learns how to fix one type of sink in one style of   house on one side of the street in one point of time, always without a solid grounding in what is essential to human relationship—the continuity of change, breakdown, rejuvenation, interdependence. People become correctional, safety, or justice specialists without any sense that their personal convictions about punishment have their foundations in the social conditions they attempt to create in their own lives. Courses are now taught more often than not from programmed texts, from which editors have purged all value statements, bought by publishers in accord with market research data which indicate what a national faculty will buy. For the student all things are taught to be equal in value. Clasping an anklet around the leg of a prisoner for electrocution is discussed as if it were on the same ethical level as clasping a pipe beneath a leaky sink. All means are regarded as equal as long as they solve the problem.

Ethics and self-determination questions become even more remote and masked when funding is sought or can be found for one's project, as life becomes a never-ending series of discrete projects.

As soon as anyone makes an attempt to question this process of specialization and licensing and introduce the necessity of a social ideal, shouts of irrelevancy or impracticality are heard. It is feverishly asserted by specialists that a social ideal serves only to confuse our sense of justice, and therefore is not "reality-based." Reality cannot be anything that is confusing or painful. However, I offer an equally plausible argument for explaining why people hold on to a strictly practical orientation, in that it is a means to avoid questions of unity, both personal and social. It is also a means to avoid personal involvement in often painful social justice issues such as the ethical dilemmas involved in the use of lethal injection (Christianson, 1979a). "The practical" must be seen as a political idiom that means personal submission to the information or worldview or standards that will get oneself or others certified, will get one through the day, through life without human involvement. It means taking the human being solely as a toolmaker, conceiving and building social tools and containers without understanding the human personality and sociality which these tools and containers are supposed to support. Human hurts are treated as if they were isolated, discrete events without any social context or historical-political base.

Spiritually, this emphasis on the practical entails limiting the search of one's soul for meaning in an almost dictatorial way, as if the tools or materials—ethical and moral—for creating safe communities could be found in an equalizing core curriculum or management technique. "The practical," therefore, can be looked upon as a kind of novocaine for numbing one's sense of reality to the risks of a free, autonomous life, to the pain that comes from the uncertainty of human relationship. By denying the importance of understanding the theoretical framework or social ideal of one's political-economic self, one can always avoid stating to oneself and to others the boundaries and depth of one's convictions. One can always remain utilitarian and chameleon-like, changing one's boundaries and ethical foundations to fit one's current supervisor's, faculty member's, journal editor's, or statesman's view of reality.

Instead of the study of human hurts, their correction and healing being a freeing experience, those who study or live "practically" become themselves imprisoned in a commodity existence, always sitting on the edge of life, peering over to see which way the ideological wind will blow. The nature of one's social ideal, the depth of one's convictions, are limited to potential placement in an agency, faculty, or research group. Only questions are asked and pursued that will facilitate mobility in the workplace.

The basic human urge to discover how we can live cooperatively as persons is traded for how professionals can protect their economic-political domains successfully.

Enlightened faculty in universities are no exception, living their lives according to tenure committee standards rather than present, often pressing, questions of social justice. Those who seek the university curriculum for credentializing soon recognize patterns they learned in earlier education experiences; they have to develop an economy of self to get through, to limit themselves to statements and projects that will have certain payoff and minimize social friction. In those who follow this course it is possible to notice a deterioration in personal values, a darkened laissez-faire insensitivity to life, embodied in a lethargic professional shuffle.

In short, rather than opening oneself up to the possibilities of self through cooperation with others, the student, the professional, learns to become part of a delivery-consumption system. The possibility of considering any alternate social reality is lost. Each person becomes his role-to-be (the more robopathic in nature, the better), whatever he or she is taught, whatever an agency or supervisor maps out as the correct view of reality. Personal values and personal consciousness, if they remain at all, are sacrificed for "society," "the future," "progress." Preparing to deliver commodities to others, a person learns to think of him or herself in terms of commodity, learns to live as a marketed commodity.

The strange irony in the vehement rejection of social theory by the group of "realists" I have been talking about is that they have a position not without an underlying theory or social ideal. In fact, it is a position with a well-defined political-economic foundation, but one that always remains "tacit and therefore unexaminable and uncorrectable" (Gouldner, 5). By denying or neglecting theory about people and how things are and should be connected in this universe, one fails to get a hold on life, for one never has a hold on one's self. Consequently this person eliminates any risk there might be in reordering his or her thinking about life. It is understandable. Those who have begun to face the risk of finding an exit from power-based economies are criticized for their search. It now seems commonplace, for example, to punch holes in the arguments of Richard Quinney without taking into account that he is one of the few criminologists to have grown up in public, to be vulnerable before the rest of us by asking questions about existence and work and social relations. Quinney may not be the best representative of Karl Marx (I believe he is too sensitive a person for that), but he is certainly the best representative of himself. If we are not sensitive to the personal struggle of each person expressing him or herself in search of meaning and justice, we will live in a generation of people who lock each other into new forms of ideological jails.

Many correctionalists who consider themselves "change agents" direct their change efforts to alter the structural forms of social life, with the hope that the character and life conceptions of others will be altered, but without any effort at personal rejuvenation. As Tolstoy notes:

This is rather like altering in various ways the position of wet wood in a fireplace. It assumes that one can place wet wood in such a position that it will catch fire. The error in this is so obvious that most of us could not submit to it if there were not a powerful reason which rendered us susceptible, for we all know that only dry wood will catch on fire independently of the position in which it is placed. Our susceptibility to this error is that the alteration of the human character must begin in ourselves, and demands much struggle and labor; whereas the alteration of the structural forms of the social life of others is attained easily, without inner effort over one's self, and has the appearance of a very important and far-reaching activity. [1919:113]

This shifting-wood approach to life has brought correctional theory to a level of inbreeding that is now counterproductive to cooperative social relations. It is not unfair to state that what has come to be known, defined, and taught as correctional theory is really nothing more than a washed-out configuration of arranged and rearranged clichés and stock phrases, an adherence to standardized codes of expression and conduct that take on the socially recognized function of protecting people from themselves and reality (Arendt). Sooner or later, for many, living comes to mean the complete denial of self, subservience to the principles of a social order that treat the human person only as a source of profit and maintenance. Human personality and sociality become farcical drama for desperate laughter. The student of corrections becomes to the correctional business what the "criminal" he controls and regulates through his commodity relation becomes to capitalism—the clientele that gives the system its definition and raison d'être.

One ought not to confuse practical orientation with a way of life in which people face their everyday concerns as they come, engage the particulars of life directly, get close to the uncertainties of experiencing humanly and living together. The practical is a way of life that avoids the particulars in exchange for abstractions (e.g., memos and standards). As I mentioned earlier, by sticking to the practical and thinking of corrections only in the context of a profession, an administrative, state-certified practicum, a person creates a good defense, an indirect way of holding on to an absolute, one-dimensional pattern of life in a well-disguised way. By treating questions of corrections as immediate administrative problems, one at a time, it appears as if one were involved in the particulars of life. However, there is no continuity in what one does, no social map or life context from which to gauge one's position. Each correctional act becomes, as it were, an individualized, privatized, discrete event, each program a singular reality with no relation to larger social questions. One's personal history becomes a "blind impersonal sequence of events over which we have no control" (Nouwen, 37). The pragmatist imprisons him or herself in a series of anonymous administrative events.

The life of the correctionalist is fraught with even greater contradictions, for while thinking that he/she can create more social justice by professionalizing, a life of doing justice to him or herself becomes even more remote. Professional requirements foster disconnectedness from the living conditions for which they exist, those diametrically opposed to what is quintessential for justice, namely, interdependence and mutuality. The "quintessential form of justice has been and is forged under conditions which make individuals increasingly interdependent: (1) aware of other's life throughout the world; (2) aware of world resource distribution and economic arrangements; (3) aware of world political interdependence; and (4) aware that ideologies and concepts of justice which promote hierarchy and the view that each can succeed on his/her own competitive or contributive worth are less plausible and in fact destructive or injurious to others" (Tifft, 1978:10). As a replacement for grasping things as connected and for living interdependently, the correctionalist chooses to become a commodity, an extension of the state-professional delivery system and through such an affiliation to remain outside his or her own history, always unaware of his or her own power to create in cooperation with others.

On a practical level, the failure to resolve or even face this contradiction can be found in the two lives correctionalists choose to live. First, their proposals for essentially administrative or managerial solutions to safety problems come at a time when many people have developed strong sentiments of anti-institutionalization. In a growing tradition of "small is beautiful," as Schumacher has illustrated, people are increasingly reluctant to give themselves up to being "managed" by any organization or social setting larger than human grasp, for fear of being swallowed up totally or duped irrevocably by impersonalism. There is a clear movement to resist, to challenge, even to avoid wherever possible what is larger than the human because of its insensitivity to human concerns. Warehouse institutions, warehouse-based ideology, are judged to be deleterious to human experience and the emergence of community, for they are hardly capable of meeting serious human needs humanly, that is, face-to-face. What is currently happening among many who call themselves revolutionists seeking to resolve this contradiction, is the throwing out of the baby with the bathwater, for in the absolute rejection of capitalism, they also reject sociality, interdependence, connectedness. New institutional structures and state forms are proposed that tend to "make us an instrument to serve its arbitrary ends, overlooking our individual purposes."

In what they refer to as their personal or private lives, correctionalists themselves are increasingly sensitive to the dehumanizing effects of centralized existence, in fact often share in bitter criticism about the interference of centralization in their lives. They are members of a community with deeply personal opinions about how these centralized, professionally managed structures thwart and strangle a person's creative aspirations, regarding people as commodities or "futures." However, what many correctionalists seem not to grasp is that in their professional lives, in their work roles, they create and maintain this very same commodity existence, and as if it were a right. Professionally they share in creating the very same social conditions they attempt to avoid or resist in their private-home lives. They support a professional, centralized delivery system that treats people as commodities and strangles them with clientele existence. The correctionalist creates for him or herself a share in the cultural schizo-existence, attempting to deliver a social unity which he or she fractures with each professional act.

It is precisely this dichotomy between private and public existence, between theory and practice, that is the greatest problem in developing theories and communities with social unity. Traditionally the dilemma has been resolved by choosing or emphasizing one or the other, theory over practice or vice versa, with the result of constructing social forms into which people are fitted, with force if necessary. Through a mutual aid alternative this problem is resolved with a practice that contains a theory of relationship, in which speaking about unity is not opposed to action but part of action toward unity.

5

PRESENT FOUNDATION OF CORRECTIONS

Addiction to the State

For anyone interested in fostering social harmony or unifying society, whether we refer to it in terms of safety, corrections, or crime reduction, the first step is to question the monopoly on healing or unifying competencies which the state and its certifying professions claim for themselves. The programs and theories that have been offered under state-scientific or scientific-professional labels, by their assumptions, by their very existence, deny that each person is humanly competent to create sociality and that communities possess the competencies for a correct world, a safe place to live.

I am not advocating that each person in the community or neighborhood, as a form of challenge to these limited definitions of what is possible, ought to begin writing a treatise on justice to get a foot in a fast-closing door, or ought to be contributing his or her part to the refinement of the latest scientific theory on corrections. Such a form of participation would be an avoidance of the basic questions that have to do with personal and community-based competencies. Rather, I am asserting that each person—outside state, scientific, professional domains—is the source of what is corrective and that the professional-state monopolization of these means or resources is only one historical, ideological derivative of what is fundamentally a universal, personal process. Once people come to grasp the meaning of this, a more meaningful approach might be for each person to pay more attention to the materials of personal competencies which have been hidden or forfeited or denied altogether in exchange for the novocaines delivered by an impersonal, commodity-based complex.

When correcting activity is treated as a commodity, as if it were a series of activities outside or superior to human activity, beyond the everyday giving and receiving activities of people in community, people begin to live behind locked doors, with ferocious chained dogs as companions to alleviate fears that, grown to monster proportions, become more annihilating than their original stimulus. Safety becomes a matter of waiting for the problems on the street to subside, to be cleared by state officials or by professionals.

But it is this very act of waiting, this consumer-based passivity on the part of people, exhibited in the abstention of their social presence and the surrendering of self to others paid to deliver social presence, that is the problem. It amounts to the denial of one's own capacity to create the conditions for sociality, and worse, the denial that one's own abstention from life might be a contributing cause of the very problems one is paying others to get rid of.

This way of approaching life becomes simply that, an approach, but not living or being. As Tifft points out:

It provides freedom from the interference of others and freedom to work with others. But while providing these freedoms against the demands of others or from a tyranny of others, it thwarts the freedom to be *with*, care *for*, and work *with*, others. Instead of supporting human caring relationships, expanding their scope and intensity, promoting interpersonal cooperation and trust, the opposite relationships are engendered. Instead of a wholeness, a oneness with the earth, nature, all, competition for personal egoistic appropriation is encouraged. [1979]

The very acts one engages in to create safety are those that help to erode social bonding and maintain the boundaries that make us strangers to each other.

This consumer-based dependency, as I have stated from the outset, is not a phenomenon singular to corrections, but is part of a larger social epidemic, our social-cultural addiction to the state. It has its roots in a capitalist service-maintenance economy. Addiction to the state for personal and social safety is of the same genre of dependency as our cultural dependency on the automobile for movement, oil for energy, the physician for health, the psychiatrist for sanity, the classroom for learning. As far as community-based competency for safety is concerned, the history of the American correctional system has been that of a continuing effort to encourage people to become more dependent upon the state-professional complex and thus continue to reinforce the need for the state in our lives—no different from the corporate advertising that encourages us to be dependent on the processed food products of agricorporations. Where are the writers today encouraging people and communities to be self-reliant, particularly with respect to safety and our caring for each other? Yet, as Daniel Berrigan notes: "Most of us can't find unpolluted air, or benevolent police, or civilized wards, or political authority that speaks in a sane way. We are really left with very little; enclaves of underdeveloped people in an underdeveloped society huddling in the night. About all we can do is refuse to be eaten" (121).

With such a dependency created, the presence of social harms, personal hurts, is not viewed as an opportunity for each of us to evaluate ourselves, our relationship to others, and our communities as needing greater solidarity and mutual aid. Rather, it is turned into requests for more police, more prisons, more secure prisons, greater doses of punishment, more state-administered drugs, more complex therapies—in short, greater reliance on the state as a tool for enhancing personal and social integration. Faced with what is part and parcel of the human condition—human misery, pain, hurts, social harms—people press the state into service as a kind of social anesthesia. We deny the responsibility we have toward each other. The result is evident; when tools become foreign and unworkable by the citizen, it creates helplessness in the citizen. As a community we have become impersonal actors, strangers in the endless drama of state control and regulation, enslaving ourselves day by day to the state and its certifying professions. Our experience of pain and hurts is turned over to another, so we never see the decaying aspects of sociality. At the same time, however, we forfeit the possibility of autonomy and self-reliance.

What seems most remarkable is that most people who have grown up in America today, in the West for that matter, even those who now reject capitalism as a means to human progress, find it impossible to imagine that there is a different way of approaching life and community other than through the presence and regulation of the state.

When we look at the *powerlessness* of the individual and the small face-to-face group in the world today and ask ourselves *why* they are powerless, we have to answer not merely that they are weak because of the vast central agglomerations of power in the modern, military-industrial state but that they are weak *because* they have surrendered their power to the state [Ward, 19].

Implied in the continuing latching on to the state for a sense of safety and security is a more fundamental belief about relationship, namely, that community is not possible on a face-to-face basis, that people must rely on something (some force or system or expertise) or someone outside themselves for community to have meaning or validity. The result of this kind of thinking has been the evolution of a culture of people less and less fit to direct their own lives, thereby reinforcing the state's claim that people are not fit to solve their own problems and require things like legislation and electronic monitoring for community safety and personal protection—a vicious cycle. There is some truth to this claim, for so many people have become so extensively bound up with the state and a commodity-based, market-intensive existence that they have lost touch with the human resources that enable them to be themselves, to have some continuity of their own with some sense of a worthwhile past. Therefore, the corollary values that project hope for a worthwhile future are lost or abandoned.

We have in effect become a disabled community, relying on a system of means (production) that profits from the disablement. State-certified schools, for example, foster ignorance by limiting learning to state-certified places and curricula. And medical practice, as Illich suggests, "sponsors sickness by reinforcing a morbid society that encourages people to become consumers of curative, preventive, industrial and environmental medicine" (1977:24). Institutional care or some contrived form of state-directed supervision, becomes a necessity, more and more justified by the state as people fall apart and break down from being locked into consumer positions all their lives.

So concerned about basic survival needs and holding themselves together are the very people most beaten down by the capitalist disposal-maintenance economy that they find it virtually impossible to engage in any direct protest against the very political-economic system that creates their hopeless conditions or to reshape the society that stigmatizes their most human efforts as dangerous. For many there is no sense that their plight is related to the political economy of an elitist-maintaining culture. For still others the dribbling rewards of the system are their only option to dull the pain of their present hopeless existence. Blindly they struggle to get a share of the power, wealth, status, control system, the very disease that fosters their cancerous hopelessness. The disposal-disabling economy is perpetuated as they begin to disable others in their consumptive journey for hope.

A good example in corrections of people who have attempted to reshape their lives can be found in the efforts of ex-prisoners who organize themselves into mutual aid groups for support after release from prison. But so beaten down by the prison experience are they, so bereft of the skills and tools for the new world of technology and economic scarcity into which they return, so excluded from employment opportunities through the cold, distanced, stigmated identity of ex-convict, that they find themselves newly imprisoned. As Hans Mattick argued (a man himself subject to these very "containment ceremonies" by the academic economic system in which he struggled to be himself):

We all feel there 'should not be' any poor and pariah classes, and it offends our sensibilities to have their existence affirmed in an undeniable way. So we label them in an offensive way and deny them their humanity: dirty, lazy, stupid, crazy bums, beggars, lunatics, and criminals; and act toward them in such a way that they will fulfill our expectations and make it difficult to escape the consequence of our so labeling them. [3]

The exiles find their options limited to returning to hide their cancerous selves in an individualized existence of competitive rituals that re-create the conditions of their hopelessness.

For many ex-prisoners protest is a near-impossibility, so fearful are they of crossing the very political system that incarcerated them. And often for good reason. In Chicago, for example, officials of the Chicago police department were engaged in undercover surveillance of ex-prisoner groups to determine the nature of their activities. One of the undercover agents acted as a research assistant on a project sponsored by the University of Illinois–Chicago Circle that attempted to provide some visibility and support for the ex-prisoner struggle (McAnany, Sullivan, Tromanhauser).

The same disabling conditions can be seen in the prison itself. When prisoners have attempted to form unions and sought a living wage for the work they do for the state, they are told by the courts that the presence of unions in the prison would only serve to "increase the burdens of administration and constitute a threat of essential discipline and control" (Christianson, 1978a:243). Prisoners are forced into perpetual idleness, into identities that receive approbation from being helplessness-based. And ironically, labor unions, themselves at one time formed to support the unorganized and downtrodden of competitive economic systems, argue that prisoners "can pose an unfair competitive advantage over free-world workers, depriving the 'honest' workers of jobs and wages" (Christianson, 1978a:247). In short, the justice complex and its supporting economic substructures is a dead end. It is structured to maintain false proportions of life, to interrupt and monitor each and every attempt of persons to stay alive and human. This situation has not changed since Kropotkin wrote: "If he (the prisoner) yields to the most human of desires, that of communication with a comrade, he is guilty of a breach of discipline" (1968b:226).

Reliance on the state to provide for community safety has more far-reaching effects than is ordinarily imagined by most people, the principal effect being the destruction of the habit or instinct of sociality. "The potential of people to deal with their human weakness, vulnerability, and uniqueness in a personal and autonomous way" (Illich, 1978:24) dissolves into a fear-ridden helplessness. As I alluded earlier, people in our present culture are so convinced of their own powerlessness to direct their own lives or influence others and the world around them that they reach a point of personal immobilization. And physicians attempt to study the pervasive depression of our age solely as personal pathology! Unresolved personal problems are viewed solely as instances of personal pathology, often with a biological base, without any reference to the conditions created by power-based institutions and the state's efforts to create dependence, from which pathology generates itself. Ignored is the fact that competitive institutions are in "the business of creating a limited, docile, scientifically conditioned human animal, completely adjusted to a purely technological environment" (Mumford, 1970:284).

What people seem unable or unwilling to grasp is that the core of our safety problem is not what the state is (e.g., an equal rights state or a socialist state) or what the state does (e.g., treats versus punishes) or the form it takes (e.g., benevolent or dictatorial) but that there is a state at all. This same obtuseness is evident with respect to understanding the nature of the classroom, medicine, the workplace, and public safety in terms of political economy. The problem of corrections, for example, is not one of whether punishment can be justified under a rehabilitative label or one of outright vengeance, or in education whether the classroom is open or closed, or in the workplace whether shops have a Human Relations code for their managers as opposed to more outright forms of tyranny. The problem relates to the fact that there is a fixed place, a contrived environment where human competency is managed, distributed, licensed from without and that the state professional complex monopolizes the power to credentialize competency. Whether it be healing, learning, or working, the notions of self-reliance and self-regulation are voided and the process of human growth is put into the hands of someone else. Creativity becomes a highly limited possibility, for one's imagination is always limited by the boundaries of an industrialized self, a marketplace self. We forfeit our own human instinct to express our needs and help each other in a face-to-face fashion.

Yet we continue to persist in the belief that taking care of ourselves is a state or institutional function and that human hurts and social harms must be healed in a state-professional, credentialized system, in a fixed place, with a fixed staff, in a fixed time frame, in a fixed emotional framework over which the state-professional representative has total direction. The difficulty with this fixing is that human growth, human fulfillment is limited to time-specific, place-specific, jargon-specific, role-specific, process-specific conditions. Healthy babies are thought to be born only in maternity wards under the expert supervision of a medical staff; educated children are thought to come only from the classrooms of state-accredited schools with state-accredited teachers; emotional difficulties are thought to be resolved only in a certified therapist's office or in a state-licensed ward; real partnering is thought to occur only in state- or church-sanctioned ceremonies, as also real separation between partners; sickness is thought to real and relieved properly only when treated in accredited hospitals through a doctor's expertise and never-emptying bag of pills; and personal harms are thought to be righted only in state court-rooms and correctional facilities.

The result is sadly comical. People travel from place to place to secure bits of their accredited humanity, sanity, health, dreams. Personal and human creativity always resides outside the soul, beyond the human sphere (now cloning takes the reproductive function out of the body!) to somewhere in the professional-institutional sphere. Human experience, which begins with mutual aid, warmth, sharing, is denied as a possibility under these conditions because someone is always in charge of the processes, determining the beginning, the end, and everything in between. All life activities are imposed from without by a non-life organization, through a mask, where nothing is negotiable or freely agreed upon, for those behind the mask cannot reveal their true essence. In the meantime the autonomous neighborhood, with competencies based within, as an acceptable way to relate is banished from consciousness.

Those concerned about the imprisonment of the entire society in an effort to control a few must take into account that the fixing of people into place, role, time frames, into high crime areas and low crime areas, has the effect of creating a society of escaping people—people escaping to safer ground, safer relationships, a safer point of view, into the endlessly changing, more intricate web of the professional. I am talking about the escape from freedom.

6

MUTUAL AID CORRECTIONS

Personal, Universal, Dream Reality

For all the fanfare about innovation in corrections in the past two decades, the models of person and relationship that professionals and methodologists use are no different from what they were two centuries ago. Either they are practical without being social or they are social without being relational. My point in this book is that mutual aid solves this problem, for it is relational and social as well as practical. It is sharing in life at the most basic level of food, shelter and clothing for all. In this way, mutual aid becomes the essence of all experience. The more limited forms of relationship, such as state corrections, must be seen in their proper perspective—that is, as one political derivative of the basically human process of mutually aiding each other.

While those who offer radical solutions from the left claim that their arguments differ from those on the right or the center, these points of view are essentially the same, for they use a starting point not based on present needs. Each of the political dimensions mentioned above presents a form of social order that determines and satisfies human needs through the competencies of people and groups outside the experience of those who express the needs. Those with the needs, therefore, become useless in aiding themselves and each other. It is believed that truth is "transmitted," that solutions to problems are "delivered," that people are "transformed," etc. Human needs are satisfied by "problem solving," packaged solutions to be consumed and digested. For most professionals the main problem in getting things to work in a community becomes a reluctant citizenry, the stubborn will of consumers. It is not thought that their own starting point with respect to experience or competency or the use of power to satisfy needs might be the problem.

If one begins with an economic framework in which human needs are assessed, defined, and regulated by institutions and professions outside the experience of those with the needs, the tools used to correct will also remain in the hands of a few who reside outside the human. In a competitive economy, whether it be merit-based or rights-based, the value of a tool comes to be not to what extent it fosters social unity, human experience, or the well being of each but to what extent it meets the projected standards of those who possess the tools or claim a monopoly over their use. If corrections is defined as a state-professional activity from the outset, then the value of correctional activity can pertain only to what the original definition allows, in this case the state-professional. But tools (Illich, 1974:20) and concepts geared toward human experience need to be measured against experience—the well being of each of us—for this is the ultimate guide, not the well being of those who possess the tools, or the efficiency of the tools, or profit. Relationship based on some principle other than "to each according to his needs or well being" (e.g. merit, works, rights) brings with it a priori truths that take precedence over experience or well being. While this approach often results in rather refined, sophisticated tools, as we see from our own industrial history, they are tools which are humanly limited and which often support social conditions in which experience decays. It does not take a very critical sense to make the assessment that in our present society every single capitalist tool is now counterproductive to human experience.

When one begins to examine the word "corrections" as it is used today, it becomes clear that it has a number of qualities that, when examined closely, can help us to clarify some basic aspects of correcting relationship, thereby opening up the possibility of community-based competencies for safety and correction. On the one hand, "corrections" is a noun and seems to refer to some object or thing. University students are heard to say: "I am majoring in corrections." But also contained in the word is a verbal quality which enables it to carry some flavor of doing or making. In this sense, correcting is a process, one which a person engages in. Used in this way, the word conveys from the outset that there is at least one person engaged in the activity. But the word is also relational and social in nature, and the correcting activity, to be completed, must have at least one other person. Correcting implies some kind of relationship or interdependence, and one that supposedly moves toward some kind of unifying experience. At its most basic level then, corrections is a concept that is capable of being as extensive as all reality, all forms and kinds of relationship. Its basic requirement is some kind of giving and receiving, in which each person shares relevant parts of self (needs and gifts) so that each grows more through unity with the whole. And ultimately, corrections is not simply limited to one set of relations, but reflects all social relations. (Moran, 45) To coin phrases like "community corrections" or "institutional corrections" or "state corrections" without this more universal sense of "corrections" is to limit one's thinking and living to its market-intensive definitions which exclude the essence of cooperation in the human struggle.

While it may sound redundant to some, corrections is ideally a process in which those in the relationship really relate. It is a relationship where a mutual alliance of some sort exists, in which people can experience who they are, not through competition and self-interest, but through the free expression and satisfaction of their needs. It should be evident that the nature of the economic context one begins with and the political milieu in which economic relations are managed, whether based on competition, state distribution, distribution according to merit, or sharing through mutual aid, sets the boundaries on what the residual corrective activity will be like. Within the competitive, self-interest framework of capitalism, where human sharing is based on a consumption-commodity foundation, it should come as no surprise that the tools of correction are based on the same consumption-commodity principle. As this form of survival of the fittest or quality of life for the few has its roots in the monopolizing multinational, it should equally be no surprise that the tools of correction are based on the monopolization-maintenance principle of the multinational.

This monopolization was solidified when correctionalists and penologists who offered scientific-professional solutions to a community drained by industrialization were listened to as if they were the ultimate source of truth. The professional was listened to with greater credence as living according to the principle of mutual aid was being replaced by living according to megamachine ethics. As personal continuity began to be swallowed up by the continuity of the megamachine, there was no longer a collectively systematic way to live, that is, by the continuity provided by mutual aid. The professionals, those who promoted a systematic way to live, a continuity for industrial survival, were listened to.

But it must be kept in mind that the very term "systematic" is loaded with economic assumptions, the very kind of assumptions I have been talking about all along. It assumes that the human person has no continuity in him or herself, that the human organism is not trustworthy, and that some method or set of constructs beyond the person, beyond the community, is required for grasping the truth about relationship (Olson, 1969:35–36).

The result of this systematic approach has been the refinement of solutions to problems methodologically, but the solutions are farther and farther from the reality they were intended to clarify, farther and farther from the human experience they were intended to enhance. The main problem today is not how objective or systematic or professional correctionalists are, how scientific or disciplined they are, or for that matter what they say, but what they assume about living together and the casual way in which they introduce the state and their self-certifying competencies as a deus ex machina into our lives.

But just as science and professionalism entered the correctional picture to give scientists and professionals the appearance of being the ultimate measure of experience, their rigorous methods and narrow boundaries have pointed to the relativity of all things and brought their own methods and statements into question. Through microscopic refinement of social relations and subsequent measurement, scientific data revealed that the healing power professionals had claimed as singularly theirs has roots in the very processes each of us uses each day to resolve our life contradictions on a face-to-face basis. This revelation has brought others, namely, that the scientific-professional is not exempt from the subjectivity and confounding variables he or she claim so methodically attempts to avoid or control. This creator of a systematic world, a world based on "objectivity," is in fact prompted by the same forces that prompt us all, is "prompted by an effort, more or less disguised or deliberate, to know things that are personally important to him; which is to say, he aims at knowing himself and the experiences he has had in his social world (his relationship to it), and at *changing* this relationship in some manner" (Gouldner, 41). We are discovering that the scientist-professional, the pinnacle of Western civilization, as Eliade notes, is on "the same level with every other man, that is to say, conditioned by the unconscious as well as by history—no longer the unique creator of a high culture, no longer the master of the world, and culturally menaced by extinction" (51).

Whether a person wishes to admit it or not, in confronting the social world about him or her, each person is confronting his or her own needs, in the form of past disappointments, present dilemmas and future hopes. I maintain that especially when it comes to issues of justice there is no such thing as an objective assessment if that process is concerned with quality of life and the well being of everyone. Statements for or against punishment, for or against professional expertise, are deeply personal statements about one's own economy of self and immediate social relations—and the more deeply personal these statements are, the more systematic they are. "In creating the man that we want to be, there is not a single one of our acts which does not at the same time create an image of man as we think he ought to be" (Sartre, 17). And the greater our search for social unity, the greater the support we provide for our ever-searching self. Living does not become more systematic or real through objectivity; only enslavement does.

In short, all statements of justice, safety, and correction are in a very real and practical way an expression of our dreams, our visions, which are intertwined with our present sense of personal worth, our beliefs about what others expect of us, our fears of failure and success, our convictions, our sense of loneliness or connectedness. For the individual, justice statements are statements about self, the public presentation of our own inner searching and struggling self for mutuality, for sanity, for creation.

When it comes to social theory or a social ideal, each of us is a theorist, a mapmaker. This is a core aspect of our humanity, not one that comes from our affiliation with scientific method or with professional certification. "All moral culture springs solely and immediately from the inner life of the soul, and can only be stimulated in human nature and never produced by external and artificial contrivances..." (Humboldt, 76,63,28). It is through the continuing awareness and expression of our dreams and visions that we map out a journey for ourselves, a life's work and the social conditions in which this work is possible, is safe. In our own unique and different ways, each of us is a Columbus, making preparations, setting sail, discovering new worlds, always celebrating a potential discovery but always weighted by the possibility that our world may be flat and we may sail off. It is only through mutual aid, through shared responsibility for realizing our dreams, through connectedness with others that we do not.

Those who insist upon a purely pragmatic approach to corrections—state-defined and professionally based—eschew their personal dreams and visions as flights of fantasy, in hope of "getting there," of making progress more quickly. They fail to recognize that the very materials, the tools that will get each of us there individually and all of us there collectively are forged from our unthwarted dreams and visions. And this will not be grasped unless the risk to live interdependently is taken. Otherwise the fear will persist that our dreams destroy, that we are the evil that must be guarded against.

These dreams provide continuity of self, the means to connectedness with others, but only when the body is itself linked to the soil, the very earth and fields we attempt to free ourselves from. That is the key paradox. Our personal connectedness or unity, our sociality, our safety come from our connectedness, with the natural world, the animal kingdom, the land and the fields that provide sustenance. Unless we are willing to rediscover our connectedness with the universe, we will never make sense of our connectedness with each other and vice versa. Our tools of production and the tools of correction will turn into even greater devouring monsters.

II

THE END OF REHABILITATION
Movement Toward Professional Tyranny

The individual must be re-created in the light of a revivified humanism which sets the value of man the unique against the vast and ominous shadow of man the composite, the predictable, which is the delight of the machine.

Loren C. Eiseley

7

THE REHABILITATION CRISIS

The Tip of the Iceberg

One of the premises I began with was that the American correctional system has never had a positive influence in healing people or integrating communities. Such a statement can easily be misunderstood and readily confused with recent disenchantment on the part of people with the effectiveness of programs based on the "rehabilitation model" of corrections. What I mean by positive influence is not model-specific—that is, applicable only to rehabilitation—but applies to all forms of correctional practice, both present and past. Healing or integration of any type cannot occur unless it stems from the immediate and ordinary experience of those who require and offer help. A short discussion of recent judgments about the rehabilitation model, the assumptions on which that model was based, and its subsequent transformation into current models of correctional practice might help to clarify what I mean by these statements.

In a recent comprehensive review of nearly all correctional programs in the United States based on the principles of rehabilitation, Robert Martinson and several colleagues came to the conclusion that nothing works. After reviewing all available observations, they concluded that "with few and isolated exceptions, the rehabilitative efforts that have been reported so far have had no appreciable effect on recidivism" (Martinson, 25). To add to the dismay of those who had committed themselves to the rehabilitation philosophy, the researchers discovered that when positive rehabilitative results could be detected—that is, when people did not "recidivate"—it was not possible to determine what kinds of activities or which correctional personnel accounted for the outcome. It was not possible to say that a given person's transformation was in any way influenced by the efforts of workers who were providing the help.

Indeed, the findings of Martinson brought to light what many working in the helping professions had concluded years earlier. The correctional system that had nearly half a century earlier modified its ideology from hard labor to medicine, and its interior from factory gray to hospital white, did not heal its patients any better than it had formed good habits in its nineteenth-century hirelings. The rehabilitative mask of love was no more effective than the mailed fist of the prison. And when the correctional patient seemed to get well, it was not possible to determine what influence, if any, the correctional medic had had on the renewed person. For that matter when a convict relapsed, it could have been induced by the medicine, the physician, or the hospital stay. In effect, the research of Martinson and others demonstrated that the correctional hospital was a system of random activities, a bed of chaos, perhaps providing the very potion that kills the ailing patient.

Though some correctionalists raised technical questions about the methods used by Martinson to draw such conclusions (Palmer), most began to reorder their thinking in search of a new justification for punishment. For many who made a living as correctionalists, taking the findings seriously was a critical step in their lives, for the findings challenged the only means correctionalists had to make themselves humanly useful in a humanly useless process. The findings struck a blow to the roots of the belief that it was possible to be humanly helpful to others through the medium of the state-professional complex. The whole question of professional-state intervention in the life of another person was no longer academic in nature. It was now a matter of conscience, of sharing in the very social harm one wished to prevent. It is not surprising that the ensuing correctional philosophy of just deserts, which I will discuss below, sought to take every possible aspect of randomness and value out of the correctional practicum.

Over a century earlier the rehabilitative ideal had been established as the correctional system's new justification for its punishing activities. It was an attempt on the part of the state to engineer the dream of reason in those who refused a life of state-defined reason, whether the person in question was defined as criminal, deviant, psychopath, revolutionary, foreign-born, or lazy. The engineers would have as a practicum benevolent treatment. Treatment would become the socially palatable way to redefine those who refused the state definition of reality.

The philosophy of determinism provided the scientific justification for the new correctional practicum. If the criminal was a sick person, rather than religiously evil, only careful scientific analysis and expert treatment of the dissenting parts of that person would lead to any cure. Besides, theology with its definitions and cures had disappointed the law

(Newman, 17-51). The basic premise of this thinking was that the criminal was a person who was propelled into irrational behavior by economic, psychological, physiological forces, of which he or she was mostly unaware, and over which, therefore, he or she had little control. Struggling to make it in life, the person who engaged in criminal behavior was a person who was helpless in the face of inner forces, the "inexorable principle" that Freud worked by, exerting its unpredictable influence upon the tattered psyche of its owner.

As methods for control and correction, the earlier forms of religious chastising and penitentiary punishment were deemed foolish by the newly enlightened correctionalists. "Treat the criminal as a patient and the crime as a disease" became commonplace. If the harmful person was unaware of his demons, helpless in the face of his own confusion, he was already punished by his ignorance and station in life. The person in question would hardly recognize the symbolic value or significance of what the state was trying to do to or for him. Deterrence, fixed sentences, juries were all inappropriate administrative measures for determining guilt and the length of state medical attention for a sick person. As Rothman notes: "The idea of rehabilitation was at odds with the stipulation that the criminal complete a predetermined and unalterable sentence. The sentencing regulations presented both inmates and officials with contradictory messages. . ." (250). The length of hospitalization of a sick person could not be determined before that person entered (was sentenced to) the ward, only when the person was well and could leave. Who could predict when a person would be sufficiently socialized, domesticated, saved, or healed? Guilt could not be construed as an open-shut case, for the criminal act was not. Criminal behavior was a complex phenomenon, and the individual would require observation, scientific diagnosis, and subsequently individualized treatment that would help him to new consciousness about self. The pathological sickness that had driven the patient to blindness would be brought to light and appropriate behavior would follow.

Rehabilitationists argued that the person who hurt other people was not of the same species as you and I, but represented a distinct reality, a twilight zone of humanity that could be reached only through the finely honed instruments of science and the expertise of the helping professions. The person accused of an offense was not simply a human person committing an irrational act but rather lived within some kind of sick, demented reality. Rejected by the new breed of diagnosticians was any thought that the criminal might be a person with an alternate reality, an alternate morality that ought to be valued in some way. Rather, the criminal was deemed undersocialized, in need of a dose of sociality which might bring him back into touch with the realm of humanity the treaters lived in and affirmed through their work (Tifft and Sullivan, 1979).

In practice the rehabilitation model boiled down to the state's adoption and application of the principles of psychiatry and psychoanalysis for its correctional clientele. Correctionalists became "treaters." They had clients, or patients, as opposed to convicts or traitors. By scientific excursions into the unconscious, the treater would attempt to discover, identify, and possibly name those parts of self that propelled people into crime and madness. Wasteful demons could be excavated, exposed, shackled in the office, and put to flight. The sick person was treated like an underground copper mine into which teams of scientists and clinicians would venture deep and often, scraping its bottom and bringing up bits of the caged beast that pressed the person into criminal service and deranged ways (Mitford, 118–37). A whole new labor force developed for and rallied around the new criminal client. Social workers, psychiatrists, chemists, schoolteachers, counselors, dentists, physicians, recreation specialists, researchers, clergy, and eager volunteers all entered the remodeled state factory as staff for the new treatment-analysis.

To get to the new correctional patient, to get him to cooperate with the new technology, officials offered economic and status inducements, commodity-rewards for participation in the organization's new schedule. A merit system was introduced by way of parole and good-time. Later there would be new careers for those who reformed, to replace the normal career the criminal had forfeited for a life of crime, deviance, or madness. There were high school equivalency diplomas, just like those awarded to normal high school students. There were free (state-appointed) lawyers, free therapies, free state-operated group homes in middle class neighborhoods to which there might never have been legitimate access on one's own. There were even offers to wipe out past convictions from one's legal-paper self, to void one's unfortunate history. All the kinds of opportunities available to the state-defined normal person, to the bulk of American society struggling to get ahead, the state, through its professionally based programs, was making available to a class of people who were literally its political enemies. Since the treatment system was based on individualized progress, freedom was issued or rationed according to privilege, according to each person's individualized conformity. Cooperative utilization of available resources, mutual aid, was unacceptable, indeed prohibited. Officials worked, as Mitford notes, "to sever the inmate's ties with his family by transferring him to some remote prison. . . he is put in isolation, deprived of mail. . . . Every effort is made to heighten his suggestibility and weaken his character structure so that his emotional responses and thought-flow will be brought under group and staff control as totally as possible" (123).

The chief focus of the rehabilitationist was therapeutic administration, techniques that would foster the successful application and reception of the new state medicine, getting the convict-turned-patient to sit still long enough so that the state official might administer the medicine, even though there was no evidence that it worked, even though it might bring further decay, both spiritual and bodily, to the patient and sooner or later to the state physicians themselves. It soon came to match earlier punishment strategies in its depletion of the competency and autonomy of others, creating an addicted clientele.

The treatment approach moved in with a whole range of political-economic assumptions that most rehabilitationists did not scrutinize or challenge, much less understand or care about. While it might seem to many not to be the case, because of the interpersonal nature of the treatment orientation, the rehabilitation like the legal model it aped assumed "that an act has either no or limited interpersonal or inter-actional precedents, that an act has an ahistorical base. The act is extracted from its series, from its social-relational context. It denies both existential meaning and authenticity. It denies the reality of cultural diversity and existential authenticity by denying the participant's meanings" (Tifft, 1979). Uprooted from the political-economic context in which acts occurred, each person in effect becomes a case, part of a caseload to be processed and managed in the language, rituals, and sentiments of professional casework. There is little or no new consciousness for anyone involved in the process, for people are deprived of their ability to satisfy their human needs in a personal way. "There is little conciliatory new consciousness, recognition of the underlying bases for the conflict, no resolve for maintaining the relationship under changed structural con-ditions" (Tifft, 1979). Should it have come as the seeming surprise it did that relationship via treatment had little meaning for those who were its objects?

Long before the findings of Martinson many correctionalists had recognized the structural limitations of the therapeutic model. They sought a wider application of the therapeutic setting which would take into account the social conditions which fostered criminality. It was another among the endless variations in reform that an administrative, discipline-based starting point helped to create. In the socially conscious 1960s correctionalists suggested a reintegration model, which I see as the starting point for corrections mentioned at the beginning of the book. Through this model the idea was to expand the scope of the person-oriented rehabilitation ideology to the social environment of the individual criminal, so as to treat not simply the pathological individual but the immediate pathology-producing social environment—the neighborhood, the peer group, the family, the school, the workplace, even related social welfare agencies that simultaneously processed and regulated (both present and potential) correctional clientele. It was an attempt at social reconstruction and community change to help prisoners be reintegrated into their communities, reducing the social stigmatization of the political-economic system that excluded them (Schrag; O'Leary and Duffee). As we shall see, because this model had no political-economic base from which to understand the production of criminal justice, it had the effect of extending the state's helping hand into every corner of the neighborhood, into every potential variation in lifestyle.

For the so-called reintegrationist, correctional activities would no longer be simply the "case-by-case" processing (O'Leary, 933) of those who had transgressed the boundaries of state-defined reality, which had characterized the more narrowly defined rehabilitation approach. Rather, correctionalists would be concerned about social as well as personal reconstruction. The focus of their activities would be with "policy development and monitoring the decisions of many others." (O'Leary, 933). Correctionalists would work with labor unions, vocational specialists, employment counselors, school officials, mental health centers, community resources—in short, all or any of officialdom that interfered with the reintegration of offenders. (Empey) Corrections began to take on a social mission, signaling the beginning of a new age of the "correctional manager," who developed and supported more refined concepts and tools of centralization, who, in effect, began to pathologize the entire neighborhood. The reintegrationist was trained to deal "more with cases than with persons; he deals with the breakdown that he can perceive in the case rather than with the complaint of the individual; he protects society's interest rather than the person's" (Illich, 1978:25).

The result was a qualitative change, the emergence of the full-blown correctionalist—the manager. The nature of the correctional practicum had changed more radically in half a decade than it ever had before, more than most people seemed to appreciate. It was "no longer the individual professional who imputes a 'need' to the individual client, but a corporate agency that imputes a need to entire classes of people and then claims the mandate to test the complete population in order to identify all who belong to the group of potential patients." (Illich, 1978:26).

For the reintegrationist crime was not an act or a complaint but an event, an event of breakdown, resulting from the social conditions of the decaying neighborhood, the traditional peer group, the traditional family, etc. It was an event that arose and was defined in the network of relationships in which the offender lived. (Empey) Whereas most correctionalists considered the reintegration philosophy a sociological broadening in scope, the consideration of crime as event was in fact a severe narrowing, for it signaled the beginning of the removal of one's person—the personal—from social policy considerations. We know that "people act, people love, people speak, people work *but people do not event.* An event simply happens and is there; all the rich dimensions of personal life have no particular relation to event" (Moran, 139). It was the end of an era in which the personal-subjective was a concern of correctionalists, exchanged for management and policy design concerns. I believe it is in fact the peculiar quality of the word "event" that attracts correctionalists to it. It is a medium by which people may gradually separate themselves from personal responsibility in correcting relationship and move toward life as management, life as managed needs, life as policy design, execution, and fulfillment.

In terms of choice of a starting point, the direction of reintegration was clear: it was more economical (fiscally, personally, emotionally) to indict the neighborhood in America, the foundation stone of autonomous community, than to challenge or modify one's position on economics, the state, and its professional system of competency production. With the emergence of the new correctional manager, the state could begin to come in through the doors, the windows, the torn roofs and cracks in the wall of the community-turned-ward. In essence, this movement toward social pathologizing was in no way different from the movement toward personal pathologizing that had taken place within the rehabilitation model. Toward the end of the nineteenth century the then correctionalists, rather than accept the fact that the prison was a destructive social tool and ought to be abolished, chose to avoid an indictment of the system and prefer one against the prisoner—as sick and diseased. "And by incarcerating the deviant and dependent, and defending the step with hyperbolic rhetoric, they discouraged—really eliminated—the search for other solutions that might have been less susceptible to abuse" (Rothman, 295).

The coming of reintegration was a high point for the socially conscious liberal—a drawing card, one might argue—for his affiliation with a state agency, when challenged, could be justified by the socially conscious elements within the model. Reintegration provided an even more enshrouding mask than rehabilitation, for beneath the aegis of social consciousness the liberal could wave the banner of sympathy for the underdog (Gouldner) and in the other shake the mailed fist of the certifying state. Whatever the intention of the Reintegrationists, they served to create greater dependency on the centralized state, on the newly emerged caretaker class, thereby helping to further disable the neighborhood, for they incessantly decried the seemingly unstructured forms of neighborhood self-regulation. The comparison was odious, for the autonomous neighborhood's abilities to regulate itself were always measured against the yardstick of the militarized, centralized existence of state bureaucracy. Gouldner saw this socially conscious liberal as a person who "produces information and theories that serve to bind the poor and the working classes to the state apparatus and to the political machinery of the Democratic Party, while, at the same time, helping the national bureaucracy to unmask the inept, archaic *local* bureaucrats and to subject them to control from the national center" (500).

The irony in this movement toward encouraging social reconstruction is striking, for when communities took this criticism of their decay seriously and began to redevelop at the neighborhood level so as to take charge of their own economic-political lives, both government and professional support were swiftly withdrawn. As community groups became "radicalized," socially conscious liberals denied their affiliation with the groups. Free and autonomous communities would be acceptable only under the control and regulation of the state, the professional and corporate funding centers. Potentially rebellious groups were soon stigmatized into oblivion through the philosophy of benign neglect, reflected in such mocking statements as Daniel Moynihan's: "It may be that the poor are never 'ready' to assume power in an advanced society; the exercise of power in an effective manner is an ability acquired through apprenticeship and seasoning" (136). Perhaps he was referring to socialization by way of advanced Harvard education or a stint in the diplomatic corps or in the United States Senate.

In retrospect, the reintegration model of corrections reflected a significant but often overlooked mutation in the continuing hybridization of correctional reform. It signaled the ushering in of a new correctional client. For the justice system, continued investment in the transformation of its century-old clientele—the criminal waif, the stranger, the dissident—was no longer a profitable venture. Prisoners, for one, were no longer on a grand scale used as a labor pool for the state to hire out for profit (M. Miller, 17). Nor were prisoners valuable as sources of data as they once were under the rehabilitation model. It was a changed economic world. Internationally, warmaking and renewal by subsidy were no longer profitable ventures as they had been several years before (e.g. Viet Nam). It was now more profitable for corporate business to invest in the state itself, domestically. The welfare-transformation state began to become the direct source of investment, but not as in its rehabilitationist or more socially conscious reintegrationist forms. Transportation, housing, education, subsidization of the colonized poor, media, mental health, environmental problems, and crime control were now marked for investment (Tifft and Sullivan, 1979). The immediate correctional client would no longer be the risky "social throwaway" in the form of the criminal, the poor, the insane, but the correctional manager and his supporting organizational structure—his support teams and technological hardware. The criminal dissenter was not a dependable client, never seeming to fully catch on to what nineteenth-century penologists desired. As Wines and Dwight noted: "What we want is to gain the will, the consent, the cooperation of these men, not to mold them into so many pieces of machinery" (178-79;181). The new client's only required asset would be an affinity for power distribution, power maintenance, life maintenance within the system.

For many people who have felt thwarted by the increasing bureaucratization and centralization in correctional administration and their offspring of impersonalism and relational distance, the negative findings on the rehabilitation model had the effect of unmasking the wizard for them, of uncovering what they had felt all along, that wearing the mask of love is not the same as giving authentic love, that mutual aid rendered as a service or commodity is not the same as mutual aid freely given on a face-to-face basis. As social relationships continued to centralize and as administration increased in size and power, the sentiment of Paul Goodman seemed truer and truer to them, that people become stupider and more careless, less caring. "Freedom of action is not only proscribed but guided, restrained, channeled, shepherded and stupefied" (Tifft, 1979). There was little hope for remaining human in correctional organizations, much less for creating human conditions for others. Martinson's findings provided an opportunity for some fundamental questioning. For some it was liberating to discover that their feeling of being imprisoned by bureaucratic procedure and rules was supported by facts outside themselves.

For the state the findings on rehabilitation were supportive of its core claims about "defective" people, that even when you treat the wicked to health and freedom, a share in the American dream through repeated opportunities, they do not respond. There must be a biological foundation to criminality which only a new and realistic approach would discern. (E. W. Wilson; Caplan).

What most people failed to grasp all along amid the debates over the demise of rehabilitation is that it makes no difference whether you beat people into submission with a baseball bat (outright punishment) or with a pillow (treatment); the effect is the same. People are being enslaved by hierarchy and a power-based, commodity orientation to living. The correction process might take on new facades or new masks of love to maintain itself amidst internal contradictions, but it was still a commodity to be thrust upon people, one that remained a monopoly of the state and its credentializing professions.

It is important to recognize, therefore, that rehabilitation was on its way to being scrapped *not* because nothing could be found that worked. Nothing ever did or could work in the inhuman, hierarchical complex that thrived on relational distance—nor was it supposed to! Such a result would defeat the whole maintenance purpose of the system. When things did work, so to speak, they were of such a nature—personal and existential—that workers had to deny their affiliation with the correctional complex and become their authentic selves. (Sullivan, Elwin, and Dexter, 30-31). These positive results were not recorded because scientific methods could not pick up their effects. The methods were concerned with "cases" and case maintenance factors. And the more sophisticated the methods became to analyze residual variance, the more elusive these human, personal, existential factors became. They were and remain beyond the system and its array of methods.

The rehabilitation ideology was being scrapped in response to changing international economics. The new form of scarcity defined by capitalist multinational economics no longer allowed for the continued investment in "benevolent incapacitation" that had infused state programs right down to the civil service system, in the form of screening, classifying training and upgrading. Benevolence as a principle of state management and professional relationship was obsolete; it had reached its maximum utility as a method for justifying the state's punishment activities (O'Connor; Krisberg, 135-36).

Once again, we do not have to limit our observations to the correctional complex. There are confirming data elsewhere. Benevolent control has been washed from the walls and curriculum of the classroom by a radical return to the three Rs, not for their value in fostering learning, but for more disciplined management of student potential. In medicine doctors have hidden themselves behind fortresses of malpractice insurance from the patient-turned-enemy. In the workplace managers have introduced the robopathic management of oneness with the organization to replace the more haphazard Human Relations school that had characterized the mid twentieth-century workplace. For the state welfare system, the emphasis would no longer be on providing jobs for the unemployed—despite the rhetoric—for now a group or colony of unemployed, of unemployable is a necessary component of late capitalism (Kalecki). A posture of providing for, once economical for an economy of growth, is now counterproductive for the emerging twenty-first-century political-economic complex. Basically the new ideology is a job, an education, health, for one's beliefs, that is, becoming one with the state. It is "the emergence, or rather the institutional specification, the baptism, as it were, of a new type of supervision—both knowledge and power—over individuals who resisted disciplinary normalization" (Foucault, 296).

Clearly then, the end of rehabilitation was not really an end in the sense that it had evolved into something else. Rather, it was a signal for the beginning of a new form of state control, one that would be direct and rooted deeply in the new economics of survival—a job for one's bread. Work would be made available in exchange for one's convictions (Coughlin, 6). As I shall discuss later, politics has become food and food politics. Those who had fought tooth and nail over the value of rehabilitation one might have expected to leave state agencies or their professions, so as to live out their convictions. Rather, what has happened has been a resentful compliance, an adjustment to the new mask of love. While it might sound to some like a harsh judgment, the new economics makes the time ripe for the state to reintroduce what I refer to as executioner or extermination bureaucracy to control those who would be critical of such a soulless practicum. The new just deserts models are a move in this direction, managerial strategies to avoid public hostility such as had flared up in the past whenever the state executioner appeared in public to take life (Takagi, 20–21).

Those who criticized the liberal position of rehabilitation for its weaknesses have not sought a new starting point for creating social unity, but continue to support administrative strategies that have their basis in an already decaying foundation. For some the mask of love is abandoned altogether for incapacitation, Martinson among them: "The realistic threat of punishment and a high degree of certainty of punishment plus restraint (resulting from surveillance), tools which we use successfully every day to control our children, our co-workers and those we encounter in the street, might be effectively used as methods for controlling *street crime* within the framework of a democratic value system" (Wilks and Martinson, 6). The seeds of a "carceral archipelago" ideology that Foucault has described are sown (Foucault,, 298–308). The economic-political context in which the crime problem is to be solved becomes clearer: it will be a totalitarian context.

8

REHABILITATION

Never a Possibility

It is important to recognize when discussing the demise of rehabilitation—whether it is referred to as treatment, reintegration, or reformation—that as a process or means of healing or making whole, via the state, it was never a possibility. There are only certain kinds of perceptions and experiences that can exist within given economic structures—the extreme being that something cannot be its opposite at the same time. But this was precisely the problem with rehabilitation, namely, that as a form of state-directed aid its underlying and necessary principle of shared responsibility for health and growth had to be sacrificed for the monopolization of the process by the state and its privatizing professions. What rehabilitation stood for at its roots—both philosophically and structurally—is diametrically opposed to the ideology, structure, and function of the state. The underlying principle of rehabilitation is that there is no human justification for punishment ever in correcting relationship, whereas the state's very existence is based on the principle that punishment is a political—and therefore human—necessity. Let me explain.

Rehabilitation as a treatment modality had its roots in the principles and processes of psychiatry and psychoanalysis. The underlying concern of these methods is "to uncover the principle of union, or communion, buried beneath the surface separation, the surface declarations of independence, the surface signs of private property" (Brown, 142) to bring about unity within a person and the unity of self with the whole, with what is other. Through the mutual exploration of dreams, the primitive, the unconscious by therapist and patient, a common humanity, a basic human goodness is confirmed, accompanied by the revelation that magic as well as madness are everywhere, are factors to be reckoned with by every person in his or her struggle to be human, throughout life, as well as by every civilization. We discover as well that sickness and health are not limited to certain age groups or to certain classes of people or to certain kinds of people biologically. Sickness is a continuing state of self, of every person struggling to be free from illusions and the meaningless of externally imposed boundaries. Similarly health is a continuing state of self, awareness that "the distinction between self and external world is not an immutable fact, but an artificial construction. It is a boundary line; like all boundaries not natural but conventional; like all boundaries, based on love and hate" (Brown, 142). Sickness and health, like love and hate, power and cooperation are ever-present in each of us simultaneously. And if competition and power are believed to be at the core of the human essence, so also then are cooperation and mutual aid equally situated at that core (Rogers, 1961). It is the existing social-economic conditions—whether they are based on principles of competition and power or cooperation and mutual aid—that brings forth and reinforces the meaningfulness and authenticity of one or the other state of self: sickness or health. When social conditions are personally supportive, based on trust and cooperation there blossoms a wholesomeness of self, where previously there had been depression, neurosis, madness, under conditions of power (Jourard). The unity or rehabilitation of a person is as possible or impossible as the unity of the "corporation soul" about him.

Through the principles of psychoanalysis we discover that at the level of the unconscious we all share the same dream of being free, as well as the same persistent despair of ever reaching that goal. Personal problems along the way may be unique to specific persons at given times, but they are not the result of a fixed, determining force which reflects a flaw in the basic nature of the human organism. If this were the case—that is, if one organism were flawed by nature—so are we all. Rather, personal problems are universal because each of us is part of a finite human community, struggling to find meaning. They are also unique because each of us finds this meaning or completion in different ways, for our needs and struggle are unique.

Healing, rehabilitating, overcoming madness, are not some thing, or object therefore; they do not emerge in what is given to one person and consumed by another, but in people being present to and supportive of each other through their own words and gestures. Healing or rehabilitation is a deeply personal experience, but it is also shared in that people begin to unmask what they were hiding, begin to break down the surface separations that kept them apart. Healing comes in the experiencing and expression of our needs among others, for through our needs we begin to recognize that each is unique but also that the needs we have are universal, belong to others, that all suffer from the weakness, vulnerability, and ignorance of the human condition. Healing, as with sickness, is an equalizing process, for it asserts the primacy of human experience as connectedness with each other. It requires the dismantling of any political-economic system that maintains ownership, separateness, and disconnectedness. Such a system is by nature anti-human, for it destroys the very process of connectedness that gives us a true sense of our humanity. Our sense of humanity may be our frailness, but it is also our strength.

The very existence and continuation of the state, on the other hand, requires the maintenance of life based on private property, class distinctions, separateness, and surface declarations. The existence of the state presupposes that the means of production (to meet human needs) is not the shared work of humanity, but that each individual creates or produces an object entirely by him or herself, having a right to appropriate it. The same is true, therefore, of sickness and health. Sickness and health are not shared or universal phenomena but are person- or group-specific—namely, for those who do not produce and who do not appropriate for themselves what they produce. The state is based upon this privatized notion of production and health, reinforces the personal pathology theme of sickness, thereby creating a place for itself as rehabilitator. All are subject to rehabilitation who are excluded from what the state defines as the essence of health—the producing, appropriating, adult, white, male. He or "it" is the standard of health, sanity, non-criminality.

State ideology asserts, therefore, under the cloak of scientific method, that Black, Indian, Hispanic, and Mexican Americans are prone to criminality, that women are prone to madness, that children are prone to delinquency and self-centeredness, and that their acts are the result of personal and group-specific pathologies, flaws they alone possess and which they alone should take responsibility for—that is, to be punished for. The schisms of age, race, sex, and class that are created and maintained by a competition-based capitalist economy are exploited by the state to justify its role as rehabilitator. Healing, providing competency, becomes the sole function of state-trained, state-licensed personnel who are willing to accept surface declarations, surface separations—that is, the political—as the fully real. Human responsibility is not responsibility to community but to consuming the state-professional concoctions of reality.

State ideology is the direct opposite of that based on shared responsibility as understood in the principles of psychoanalysis. For the state then to take on rehabilitation as a way to foster social unity is an impossibility, for the means as well as the consequences of rehabilitation do not permit any externally imposed conditions on experience. Healing, personal and social unity, become an impossibility when one part of the healing relationship claims a monopoly over the definition and process of authenticity or remains a constant or absolute. Personal autonomy or healing is fostered only when both partners move toward the full engagement of themselves. And since, in human interactions, each is partly enveloped by the experience, neither can presume to have a monopoly over the entire interaction. Nothing is more destructive of a relationship of two persons or groups, nothing inhibits helping or growing more, than the assumption that one of them is at a fixed point trying to move the other. When this superior-inferior, mover-moved relationship exists, only frail identities emerge and are reinforced. People do in fact lack the power to heal or grow. Why should continuing recidivism ever be a surprise when such conditions are maintained? These are the social conditions the state fosters, for the state is an abstraction, an unmoved-mover, a blind tool, limited by the economy it serves.

The state in fact becomes the producer of pathology and disablement, for it assumes an absolute position, a position outside the relationship it directs, ordering all involved to order themselves in such a way that the state remains central. We should have learned from the life of Copernicus the utter foolishness of such a fixation! Personal dreams, personal realities, may exist outside the state, but they are not valid realities until certified by the state. Therefore those who would engage in the state's brand of healing or integration, whether it be called rehabilitation or reintegration or any of their modern counterparts, must deny their own connectedness with humanity, their own participation in humankind. But for humankind "the goal cannot be the elimination of magical thinking, or madness; the goal can only be conscious magic, or conscious madness; conscious mastery of these fires. And dreaming while awake" (Brown, 254). This can occur only when competency is based in those people, communities, organisms, who have need of that which the competency will bring. Means are ends.

9

THE EMERGING JUSTICE
INDUSTRIAL COMPLEX

What should disturb us most as a society is that among the myths about rehabilitation and its various updated versions, there has sprung up a justice-industrial complex, a domestic conglomerate that serves the state in the same way that the military-industrial complex serves the capitalist economy internationally (Platt and Takagi, 2-3; Pepinsky, 1978; Mitford, 169-88). As the capitalist economy was once highly dependent on arms making, arms selling, and warmaking as sources of employment, growth, and profit, it is now increasingly dependent upon the growth, development, and refinement of a domestic caretaker class and its services delivery system.

This caretaker class that began to develop in corrections within the context of the reintegration philosophy, has developed into a highly sophisticated form in the person of the correctionalist, the corrections—criminal justice worker, a safety specialist in control, monitoring, incapacitating other human beings (Barkdull, 3-8; Van den Haag, 241-61). The marketable skills of the correctionalist change from those of rehabilitator to incapacitator. The basic job specification for being accepted into the complex is that one abide by the absolute authority of the state and its certifying professions to perform its incapacitating function, which is to "evaluate the loyalty risk in a citizen and then extinguish his private sphere" (Illich, 1978:26). Those who affix themselves to the state become the managers of the new state-directed, profession-controlling bureaucracy ghettos, an organizational version of the geographic ghettos we are all familiar with. For a "normalized" way out or up a person must rely on the very structure and professions for competency that require people to stay in and down. Our culture increasingly reflects this double bind in its peculiar brand of schizo-existence, people constantly torn between being in and getting out.

This caretaker class, whom I refer to as correctionalists or statecrats, represents the post-welfare state's version of the early twentieth-century welfare state's archetypal social worker. Whereas under the philosophy of the traditional welfare state correctional rehabilitationists were paid to process—to resocialize, reassign, retool, rehabilitate, reallocate, retrench—the new correctional manager is paid to colonize and maintain. The new justice models, which are really updated versions of old justice models, are a way to mask the intensification of state activity. The social services complex, for example, has its income-maintenance units to maintain a group of people at a less-than-subsistence level of life; the drug addiction services provide free methadone to maintain a clientele that the state can monitor easily, which it is unable to do if the drug users are on the streets competing for their supplies in a free enterprise market. As the multinational economy emerges in its more advanced forms, the creation and maintenance of a clientele of unemployed, the neurotic, the dangerous, the chemically addicted, those whom James Wilson might refer to as "the wicked," is more supportive of the economy than their transformation and return to normalcy. Enough Americans are already on drugs to make this a reality now, all looking to the state for their daily rations of reality novocaines.

The welfare state that the upwardly mobile middle class person criticizes for its "do-gooder" policies, for coddling "the lazy," "the sick," "the deviant," is now meeting the needs of these critics of welfare economics in the form of domestic concentration camps, bureaucratic ghettos, colonies of sickness. For those who continue to think of corrections or welfare assistance as a friendly, helping hand, as it was a generation ago, I urge greater familiarity with the changing assumptions of the organizations for which they pay taxes.

Each member of the caretaker class must now have an economic self-interest or personal stake in the maintenance of the sick, the dangerous, the wicked, in their disablement and disposal, for their own economic future is dependent upon quota-maintenance strategies, upon their ability to ghettoize and maintain. In a tight job market community groups must be transformed into clients to insure work. As I have mentioned repeatedly, by this practice the neighborhood is turned into a ward. The concept of "zero-based" budgeting that has become popular among governmental officials has the effect of encouraging agency officials to drum up clientele to support their jobs, to find or invent new hybridized forms of deviancy and craziness to keep them in work. Any new form of ideology, any stirring in prisons, any public dissatisfaction, is dramatized by professional groups and their unions, each and every social inconvenience seen as continuing justification for more intensive state intervention, more managers, more maintenance.

The caretaker class had in effect become a core of safety specialists with unions and professional organizations as support groups that prey upon human fears and lobby for laws that impute pathology to persons and groups. It is a business, with entire classes of people identified as valuable raw materials to be scientifically screened, assessed, gathered for processing, washed, processed, and disabled. The modern beginnings of the caretaker class were first evident nearly a decade ago in the proposals Dr. Hutschnecker offered (1970:76-77). Hutschnecker proposed a nationwide delinquency prevention program in which every six or seven-year-old child in the country would be given a battery of psychological (i.e., neurotic or delinquency prediction) tests to determine predisposition or inclination toward criminality. The proposal included special school tracts or internment camps, special adjustment camps for those who showed an unfavorable prognosis. Intensive care of persons by the state at an early age would guarantee a ward of the state for life, a steady, never-ending clientele. Children would grow up knowing only the mask of love, and perhaps face-to-face love would disappear. Hutschnecker's plan was just one of many attempts to draft children into state service, as adults are drafted into the military. The New York State Division for Youth is based on a similar philosophy. Children must "earn" their sanity or disposition to goodness—that is, learn to live according to the standards of the state rather than by human standards. Their progress is always measured against the more sane or the more just population, those already certified by the state complex, those already doing the screening, assessing, providing.

Evidence of the enormous growth of this caretaker class can be seen throughout the entire criminal justice system. For example, in 1971 the criminal justice labor force in America grew to more than 1 percent of the total American labor force. (National, 18). In 1973 the American criminal justice worker passed the million mark and whereas from 1970 to 1974 the total American labor force grew just over 8 percent, the criminal justice labor force grew more than 28 percent (U.S. Census, 1974:156). Similar statistics exist for "justice architecture" and prison populations. In 1977 over nine hundred prison and jail construction projects were at various stages of completion, a trend consistent with the 44 percent increase of prisoners from 1973 to the end of 1976 (Christianson, 1978b:146). What is most interesting is the new forms of justice subsidization. The justice system now underwrites construction costs for such projects as the Winter Olympic Games (Lake Placid) so as to take over the abandoned dormitories for a prison complex (Christianson, 1979b).

While some people might argue that statistics such as these refer to criminal justice generally, not corrections, I contend that it is now possible to equate the entire criminal justice system with correctionalism. As mentioned at the outset, rather than the criminal justice worker turning into the traditional "enforcement" person, all are being transformed into correctionalists. Police run about with correctional techniques (e.g. behavior modification) to medicate citizens when complaints are made (Somodevilla). Social workers dot the sides and back rooms of police stations to give persons taken into custody a service option—the therapist in the back room—or a justice option, the jail (Treger). Force and help, sanity and coercion become interchangeable, both conceptually and in practice.

When growth is inhibited by fiscal constraints, new forms of increase are generated. The volunteer program is one example. Volunteer groups have come to comprise a kind of community-based monitoring class, people bored with their consumer existence, zealous to be of service to the state complex. It seems that for many a meaningful neighborhood-based existence can be found only in monitoring the lifestyles of their neighbors. A report by the National Association of Volunteers in Criminal Justice computes the number of people volunteering in criminal justice agencies nationally to be 750,000, nearly equaling in number the officially paid staff. In New York State correctional organizations have over six thousand volunteers. New York State Probation Departments have nearly one thousand volunteer workers, in 1977 alone providing the state with 65,000 hours of help.

These people, extensions of the state, often pass themselves off as friends and concerned neighbors, helping to create and maintain greater dependence on the state, often able to secure a level of intimacy with state clientele which paid correctionalists cannot. All citizens are encouraged to support state-professional programs (e.g., report suspicious activities in the neighborhood) rather than develop neighborhoods of friends, or at least of people who work cooperatively in resolving neighborhood problems. People accede to these proposals, for their only interest in the neighborhood is in maintaining a residence, not in creating community. They work elsewhere; their children are bused elsewhere to school. The volunteer program and the continual urging of the state that people become part of the state is part of a larger social-economic philosophy to professionalize not only clients but also the entire citizenry. In a sense, the state simply reflects a way we have come to relate to each other—indirectly, hierarchically; professionally. This reflects a breakdown in face-to-face existence, where neighbors mutually aid each other as neighbors.

Increasingly, through the media the correctional caretaker class promotes scare ideology. They claim that only the correctional complex is effective in controlling the dangerous, that it is necessary for community safety, and that each community must have the latest in the professional control expert, the safety specialist, to meet head-on the new hybrid forms of pathology that continue to emerge. Whereas once these pathological problems were brought to the hospital, the prison, the asylum, the office, there is no longer enough room or enough professional attention to go around. Neighborhoods—the hope of autonomous community—are turned into wards with multi-disciplinary criminal justice teams of all sorts patrolling the sick beds.

The effect of all this is that those who have been ghettoized in neighborhoods, in families, in schools, find themselves now ghettoized on a second level, by the complex of state bureaucracies, competing openly for the sick and weak so as to deliver their needed services, so as to meet the quotas of next year's zero-based budgeting. Benign neglect has been replaced by powerful domain fights for clientele by state agency officials, comparable in many ways to the annual membership drive of private organizations. Might we call it a measured maintenance ideology? State agencies are divided up, expanded, given new titles, as state officials prepare new justifications for expanding their domains, increasing their clientele, arguing that the form of disablement presently maintained in Department X fits better (more economically) into the ideological specifications of their own Department Y, requiring their special brand of regulation expertise. Is not the history of getting rid of status offenses for juveniles, then reintroducing them, essentially a budget fight between the social services and juvenile courts over the control of scarce jobs?

Clients are shifted about, as if they were pawns in a game of musical chairs. In the meantime, for an extraordinary large number of economically disabled Americans, the state has become an umbilical cord, their only conceived source of survival. They journey in a twilight zone of rooms and offices, through which they move riddled with fears, from this department to that department, from division to division, reception area to reception area, waiting room to waiting room, waiting most of their lives, living some or all of their lives as official clientele, until they are judged ready to pass the minimum moral standards of the society—standards that define not a human being but an industrially—customized person, like a suit to be worn, a car to be driven. The state's personnel act as hybridized offspring of Henry Higgins, breathlessly devising new methods to modify their captive Pygmalions into suitable social masks, to be paraded before the royalty of American elites, who have no interest in them except as sources of profit, their own status maintenance, and tax writeoffs. The clientele are much like purchased futures.

With the new caretaker class there has emerged a new caretaken class, a class of people who in Pavlovian fashion report to the state every ache and ill and suspicion to be treated for free. Such irony. We see broken bodies and fractured spirits sitting hours in waiting chambers, to be divided some more by the fracturing procedures of bureaucracy—the state specialists dividing the human person's struggle into mental health, education problems, drug abuse problems, correctional-safety problems, welfare-subsistence problems, old age problems, youth problems, handicapped problems, retarded problems, etc., etc., etc.

This specialization is so concretized in people's minds that mental health problems are treated as if they have no political-economic base. Sudden depression is treated as if it is unrelated to the constant battering of a competitive, hierarchically based economic system that requires a segment of the population to be unemployed, sick, deviant, criminal, that requires a family structure with women subservient to their male counterparts, with children and older people treated as property, all valued only for their ability to fill consumptive roles. And since the old will have no more productive potential, their consumption is regarded as a social and economic liability. They are put out of sight into low budget, low maintenance, senior citizen centers. Their stories, their bodies become institutionalized in the archives of the old age home.

It is rarely conceived that what are termed mental health problems are related to having a life's work that is meaningful, secure, and human, to having a standing in a family or school or society that is dignified because one shares in humanity and not because one earns or "deserves" or produces in amounts proportionate to what one consumes. Nor do the state correctionalists consider that the repressive strategies of the workplace translate themselves into alcohol and drug use and into the battering of wives or that battered wives translate their own forms of self-destruction into the battering of their children as if to destroy them young, warning them that this life is one of despair and ignominy. The children need no encouragement; they turn to heavy drug use, alcohol consumption, and suicide as the only meaningful life alternatives. Their dreams ooze a blackened sickness, a wild but sullen desperation as they prepare to become wards of the next generation of statecrats.

The state fails to deal with the sources of the fragmentation, the battering and violence, because its own existence is dependent upon the continued fracturing and violence, in fact prosecutes those who engage in violence because the state itself demands a monopoly over processing violence. And as with any select private organization, those who choose to hang on to the state for survival pay their membership dues. In order to be a recipient of the state's beneficence, each must accept a definition of self and humanity that accepts one's problems as private, that is, as strictly one's own and due to a personal pathology.

10

LIBERAL DESPAIR

The Panic to Save Face

With the emergence of multinational, new realism economics, traditional forms of benevolence (e.g., liberalism) become too costly, and in fact unnecessary, for creating and maintaining a clientele. The liberal, the traditional standard bearer of benevolence—with one foot in officialdom and the other in the community—becomes too costly a dinosaur, involving too large an expenditure for the support and maintenance of multinational living. With a shortage of jobs, loyalty to the organization can be more easily secured from workers as a price for employment without benevolent overtures toward a clientele: "I pledge allegiance to the state and its pervasive hold over my life!" is not a different phenomenon from that described earlier for loyal clients.

For most thinking liberals these new economic conditions have shifted the axis by which they could previously have loyalties to both state and community. The changes in corrections, which most fail or refuse to recognize as having an economic base, they prefer to believe are rooted in the failure of rehabilitation. Despair and confusion overshadow their lives. The foundations on which their work lives were based are shattered. They are faced with the realization that the mask of love, bureaucratic care in its most humane form—rehabilitation—to which they had committed themselves in earnest, is not a substitute for love itself. Many have come to recognize that enforced care is not the same as the care generated through the warmth of human sharing in a direct way. Moreover, their despair reflects the pain in coming to grips with the increasingly imminent choice for either state-directed communities or mutual aid communities as the foundation for their living together.

Caught in this bind, many liberals have not been without their carpetbag of regenerative reforms. Many, unable to accept mutual aid as a practical reality in their lives, have begun to accept the state as central, but not without a reformed justification for punishment, a justification that includes their own compromised consciences. The movement of the past several years has been, therefore, to develop models of a just state or a more fair-appearing state, thereby easing the guilt or sense of self-betrayal for those who have chosen the primacy of the state over the primacy of self-reliance and community-based competencies. A more just-appearing state makes their choice seem more ethical. Their new forms of work will be mainly delivering justice (punishment) to those who deserve it. There is no ethical considerations involved in their acts, for the state is fully ethical. They simply give people their due, what is already due them from a newly justified state.

One example of the dilemmas I am talking about, and the subsequent shift in affiliation to the state, can be found among the members of the Report of the Committee for the Study of Incarceration (Von Hirsch), which in many ways reflects the life choices of liberals throughout America today. The committee, a group of over fifteen correctionalists, having come to the conclusion that rehabilitation was a failure, introduced the seeds of a just deserts model of corrections, which I refer to as a due process vengeance model, which the committee members admitted—and somewhat ashamedly—was based on a principle of "lesser harm." It was a model of fixed sentences based on the principle that criminal offenders should be punished according to what they deserve, according to the nature of the crime. Enter Beccaria Two. They concluded their report by stating: "The principles we advocate will do less mischief and per-petuate less inequity than the system with which we now live." It was a model of justice by which the streets of the decaying correctional system might be swept a bit cleaner and permit committee members—newly exiled liberals—to stroll without compromise, without troubled con-science, among the seemingly thoughtless state robopaths.

Such a solution of lesser harm is much like putting half a muzzle on a mad dog, so as to reduce by half the dog's rampant chewing into the flesh of one's neighbors. For the committee it was an act of desperation: "Our solution is one of despair, not hope." But it was a despair not faced squarely for the human possibilities, the freedom that lay within. Rather than face the issues of social justice that they alluded to in their closing remarks, they limited themselves to questions of law, the state, a capitalist economy, scientific methodology. They seem to have limited themselves to only those questions that would help them mold their consciences to fit the ideology of a twenty-first-century state (Greenberg). Rather than begin to face personal value choices that come with a new kind of starting point, however flimsily, the members of the committee hid within the safety of the group ethic, resorting to one more refinement, one more hybridized form of the punishing state, one more step toward a purified, total state. What was most significant to me was that they reinforced the prevailing state ideology that all require state-political intervention in their lives, now even the publicly despairing liberal scientific community which the state had so long struggled to coopt.

What becomes most evident in reading between the lines in such a report is that as long as one state agency or one speck of state ideology exists, it will appear not only as a thread but also as an apron string or umbilical cord for people to clutch in order to avoid personal responsibility for life. People who cannot grasp this do not understand the meaning, the essence of autonomy and freedom, much less the essence of the human struggle. We may all be born wards of the state in our present society, but our struggle, collectively and individually, is to become human, to free ourselves from the other by engaging in face-to-face intimacy with that other.

I am not criticizing the committee or liberals generally for finding themselves confronted with confusion or despair. To some extent this is a rather healthy sign, for, as Camus argues, the only real and serious philosophical question is that of suicide (3) when we doubt our humanity, our personal worth, and come to grips with our limitations, opening ourselves up to new possibilities. And though the despair may not mean imminent personal suicide for everyone, it is a sign that people have reached the end of their theoretical ropes, the various fashions of the mask of love that permitted them to survive in a culture as it once was.

What continues to be most disturbing is that the committee and liberals who find themselves in this confusion and despair are unwilling to accept their own personal struggle, their own present hopelessness, as a starting point. Rather what seems to be the result is greater divisions into left and right, where there is an almost blind heralding of abstract ideological positions that avoid present human struggle. Questions of social unity are blotted from consciousness, at least questions that begin in the present. I find among correctionalists an almost uncontrollable willfulness to produce justice or a revolution, the very willfulness that fosters the neurotic, desperate, dependent conditions for which the state justifies its intervention. Refusing to take human needs, the well being of each person as a starting point, correctionalists continue to serve the principles of an economy "for which we will continue to justify the starving of our cities, the lack of investment in basic human needs and the abandonment of the 'unemployable'—the elderly, the young, the poor, the disadvantaged minorities and the nonproducers in the name of national security"

(Barnet, 34) or community safety or professional expertise. As I have argued throughout, the justification for acting may change, but the economic and political realities remain the same. Human misery accumulates, bringing with it a despair for many at the level of food, work, and shelter, a despair far removed from the thoughts of blue ribbon committees grappling with academically approvable paradigms of justice.

11

SYSTEM RENEGADES

The Superprofessionals

As the state begins to totalize, official efforts are being made to control the independence which professionals historically have maintained as a necessary component of their trades. All independent forms of expertise are increasingly being herded within the domain of the unifying state. But like small shopkeepers of the past, professionals continue to argue for essentially free enterprise in the trade of delivering services, rejecting intrusion by the state. At the same time they also reject any alternate economic view of how to live cooperatively. Many of these protestors claim to be radical "because (1) they advise consumers against the interests of the majority of their peers; (2) they tutor laymen on how to behave on hospital, university, or police governing boards, and (3) they occasionally testify to legislative committees on the uselessness of procedures proposed by the professions and demanded by the public" (Illich, 1978:48–49).

A number of correctionalists, with a mixture of advanced academic credentials and practical experience in the field, have turned toward a form of public self-criticism, asserting that the correctional complex and their colleagues produce more rhetoric than reality. David Fogel, for example, argues that "preachers and teachers and treaters have not produced a payoff equal to their rhetoric" (180). These correctionalists see, as Fogel continues, "few enthusiasts left in prison" who are committed to their work. With a strong sense of urgency and immediacy, these self-policing professionals attribute the beaten spirits of correctionalists to personal weakness and pathology, to "inertia and smug indifference." This new more intense breed of pragmatists have become system "renegades, arguing for a new era of managerial control, which I refer to as superprofessionalism, the system's response to marxist proposals. Such a position allows these correctionalists to stand apart from the crumbling foundations of traditional professional positions (e.g., rehabilitation), avoid the tentacles of the expanding-unifying state, and reject new kinds of starting points.

On one hand, the superprofessional expresses strong criticism for those who expound "utopian diagrams about abstract justice" (Cahn, 10-11). As theories from Marxist and anarchist perspectives gain a receptive audience, the principles on which these revolutionary perspectives are based threaten the status of the new self-contained professionalism, by claiming the need for a reconstituted society in which economics, scarcity, needs are a primary concern. The superprofessional argues that what is needed is not new concepts of justice or freedom worked out within a social-economic framework but "the active process of remedying or preventing what would arouse the 'sense of injustice' " (Cahn, 10-11). One ought to be doing justice, not simply talking about it, as Fogel argues: "We can no longer await the refinement of theories before acting to modernize the field. Theorists, unlike convicts, are not quite so desperate but, like them have plenty of time. Correctional administrators are not at such leisure" (182). What the pragmatic correctionalist has asserted ad nauseam for over a century, the superprofessional reinforces adamantly: "Theory is simply a substitute for doing!"

At the same time, however, the system as presently structured has forfeited its opportunity to do justice. Legislative processes are slow, bureaucratic procedures are inefficient and unreliable for carrying out legislative intent. To do justice one has to take things into one's own hands, be a trouble shooter for an ailing system.

Like the pragmatists I discussed in part one, the superprofessional is caught in the logical but not very real distinction between speaking and doing. One might ask, if doing is so much more essential than speaking in abstractions, why more efforts are not directed at community-based competencies, why so much time is spent in fortifying competencies that have their foundation outside community, in abstract management systems. The superprofessional, in effect, is arguing not against the injustice of management systems but to maintain the domain of his or her profession, which the state is intruding upon. The claim is made: "I have the expertise to give treatment. I, therefore, have the right to give treatment. Expertise is truth, expertise bestows rights." By arguing for the rights of the helpless to consume justice, they are at the same time claiming a right for themselves to produce that justice for the helpless consuming citizenry. Arguing for the right to treatment, the right to justice, equal rights, they reinforce their own administrative producer positions, as containing the expertise and therefore the right to provide equality—that is, service equality, commodity equality.

These hybrid professionals propose as their means to justice discretionless management and sound public administration, via fixed forms of punishment. All the rights-based theories boil down to attempts to purge the state-professional practice of the discretion that had been argued over for decades by lawyers, criminologists, and correctionalists. The superprofessional argues that by narrowing, monitoring, and constantly reviewing the behavior of the correctionalist—who is first informed with superprofessional expertise—it is possible to "free corrections from its rhetoric of devilishness" (Fogel, 188).

The new models of justice are couched in terms of consumerism and consumer rights, to protect the helpless. "Consumer" (Casper), or "justice" (Studt, Messinger, and Wilson), or "civilian" (Cahn and Cahn) models are to replace imperial or official or military perspectives that have dominated the correctional complex and made it impossible to do anything meaningful for clients (Cahn and Cahn). The major concern of correctionalists, the superprofessional asserts, has to be "less with the administration of justice and more. . .with the justice of administration" (Fogel, xv).

The superprofessional ethic is based on the belief that if the state and its ancillary corps of independent professionals are to be seen as just, are to be just, they must punish equitably, which means professionally, scientifically. The state can no longer exhibit the ragged hesitancy it did in the guise of the correctional liberal—the proverbial do-gooder who never quite seemed to resolve the traditional treatment-custody dilemma (Powelson and Bendix). If anything, the liberal had projected a poor image of professional competency in taking sides on this question and would be discouraged from struggling with confused consciences in public. A new image, through essentially scientific administration, had to be brought before the tired eyes of an increasingly informed public. To a large extent it was an open, if indirect, admission on the part of those who had thought of themselves as liberals at one time, that in fact the function of the state is to punish and incapacitate. The goal of the superprofessional is not to punish less or to challenge the state as a tool for correcting, but to punish better, with more style, superprofessionally, with a more refined, equitable-looking mask of love.

In short, the new professional urges others to assist in purifying or perfecting the state punishment apparatus, by purging the system of the inept or having them adhere rigidly to professional standards, the principles of good public administration. There would then be accountability "from all processors, even the 'pure of heart'" (Fogel, 192). Regardless of the political-economic foundations of the state punishment complex, the calling card of the superprofessional would be the application of scientific method or managerial professionalism to administration, to one's means, regardless of one's ends! The new state complex, with its core of elite superprofessionals, had become the justifying Ahab Melville had depicted: "All my means are sane, my motive and my object mad."

While to many the justice-consumer models of punishment seemed to be a well-thought-out radical departure from the seemingly chaotic mess of "indeterminism" and individualism, I see them to be in reality predictable responses to changes in market relations—both domestic and international—and it is only in these economic shifts that some sense can be made of these new justice models. First, the market structures of entrepreneurial and corporate capitalism based on the principle "to each according to his merit or works" were severely undercut by multinational and state capitalism. Market relations that gave birth to the rehabilitation-treatment-liberal era had changed. Now "professionalism, bureaucratization, administration, and centralization have entangled most working persons in a web of organized subordination and non-market relations. . . . Social good is said to result from rational coordination, management, and design created by elite mandarins. . . . The concept of justice as 'the protection of established rights' is reintroduced. . ." (Tifft, 1978).

While the superprofessional attempts to find new social consciousness within his or her present struggle, it is a consciousness limited only to fortifying a system of law and a new form of state professionalism—a maintenance class—of which they are a part, a class that denies face-to-face presence to others or rations presence to those who claim a right to it. The practical concerns of the superprofessional are not human needs or the well being of each person or the expansion of new consciousness, but the narrowing of the working framework of the state correctionalist to the proportions of a robopath. All work, all feelings, all human sentiments, even one's heart, are to be overseen by managers who live by documented procedures, the job specifications of the twenty-first-century statecrat.

This superprofessional movement in effect attempts to reform the correctional system and society by purifying and controlling the political power strategies that run rampant in bureaucracy. The superprofessional argues for the substitution of one decaying political ethic for another, a more purified ethic, but one of the same genre as rehabilitation and reintegration. It is not an unlikely or unexpected system response to compete with the marxist determination for a purified state by political revolution. Both groups seem unaware that radical transformation "cannot be accomplished by political embodiment. . . ," as Gouldner points out;

"the old society is not held together by force and violence, or expedience and prudence. The old society maintains itself through theories and ideologies that establish its hegemony over the minds of men, who therefore do not merely bite their tongues but submit to it willingly" (5). This is consistent with the premise I began with, namely, that no solution to human hurts is relevant to the human struggle unless it is grounded in the lives and experiences of those who experience the problems and unless these latter share in and are in charge of finding meaning from them. The professional cannot accept this premise and remain among the professional elite, for his or her professional affiliation is dependent upon the hierarchical ordering of problems, needs, and solutions—triage—and a monopoly over the credentializing ceremonies and procedures for resolving differences.

12

VIGILANTE CORRECTIONS

The Massachusetts Experiment

For some superprofessionals the signs of the demise of rehabilitation came to be looked upon as a way to institute a form of correctional Naderism. The rampant confusion over which theoretical direction to take was seen by some as an opportunity for direct action administratively. If it was not possible to make the political trains of the correctional complex run on time, it might be possible to dismantle the railroads. When lagging correctionalists could not be convinced of the utility of the professional ethic for doing business, some professionals resorted to action based on a superprofessional ethic, some of which emerged in what I see as vigilante corrections. In a kind of modern Zorro or Robin Hood Fashion, indignant professionals would begin to challenge the power of those who treated state wards inhumanly, without concern for the needs of the latter. It was a way to beat the system in a sort of enfant terrible fashion!

Perhaps the most widely publicized example of vigilante corrections has been the radical reform Jerome Miller began in 1969, the then Director of Youth Services in Massachusetts. Appointed in October of that year, Miller sought to humanize the services for youth (e.g., no locks or hand-cuffs) and to create a more therapeutic climate within existing institutions (e.g., staff development, an open expression of feelings). He believed that the needs of the children were to be given priority, rather than administrative orderliness or staff prerogatives. But unable to apply the radical-professional ethic successfully to a system of decaying walls and procedures as well as political patronage in the juvenile training school system in Massachusetts, Miller began to shut down (what is ironic is that it was done both legally and within the acceptable framework of bureaucratic procedures) the entire juvenile training complex. Instant correctional Naderism was born (Ohlin, Coates and Miller).

While there is a tendency on the part of many people to laud this kind of administrative coup, one ought to consider that, in terms of means-ends, it is essentially another among many power-coercive attempts to effect change by professionals from the top down. The moves reflect hierarchical thinking. As far as the activities themselves are concerned, I see them as no different from the power-coercive, situational-ethic morality of the state. They reflect the same encapsulation of humans as the training school did. As juveniles walked along the streets of Boston and Cambridge, they still did not experience a sense of community as human support for their struggle to grow up in a society that profits from juvenile misbehavior. This is most clearly evident from the behavior of institutional staff on the payroll, who, Miller himself relates, refused to take just one youth into their homes, with full pay. What would these similarly thinking people, at a distance, have to offer the youth as they walked the streets of Roxbury and Framingham? Did not the lives of these workers and those of the children battered by a consumption economy have the same basis—family and community estrangement?

To make some sense of the value of Miller's strategies, we must go beyond the issues most often debated by correctionalists (e.g., recidivism rates) and answer the following questions practically. What hope was there for reintegrating the struggling young into communities when in fact no sense of community existed? Into communities that valued the young only as a source of consumption, not to be heard or seen otherwise? What did the closing of the institutions do to face directly the contradictions of the power-coercive activities of the centralized state? Did not Miller and his associates by their actions make a strong statement that monopolized power does in fact work and is most effective when it is used quickly and furtively? Did not Miller's strategies bring hope for the state's continuation, by demonstrating that the slow struggle for community is too easily abandoned for power strategies? Did Miller himself possibly hope that community might be rejuvenated, stimulated, or reborn through the surreptitious closing of the institutions, the symbols that the state is the oppressor to be dealt with?

The fact is that Miller's actions and the actions of the superprofessional generally reinforce state ideology, which claims that families are helpless to reclaim and provide for their children, that communities and neighborhoods are inept in taking charge of their own social problems. Miller's actions reinforce state ideology that the correction of social harms must be a state-directed phenomenon or a phenomenon of the power professionals, especially of those who can seize the reins of state power for their own politically defined ends. These kinds of activities ignore the fact that corrections is a universal phenomenon, that it exists in people and communities who have charge of their own destinies, their own economic, political, and social fates.

Miller's actions reassure us that getting rid of the institutions of the state in one's life or community does not solve the problem of human meaning. For those theologians who had developed a "death of God" theology a decade earlier, there was little evidence of people living together more harmoniously in the church; in fact, there was greater confusion. Revolution that persists in getting rid of soon becomes abstract and ideological, a one-time-hit-and-miss phenomenon, an event in which the human elements have been abstracted. To dospose of, to get rid of, is to emulate state tactics, which are disable-disposal tactics, geared for getting rid of what exists outside its domain. These tactics when done for the most humane purposes are still an enhancement of the state, for they reinforce the primacy of power as the most effective relational tool.

13

A NOTE ON ABOLITION

Jerome Miller's actions can be seen as providing an added stimulus for an already growing prison abolition movement in America. Prison abolitionists have been courageous in citing the effect of the destruction of the prison on human beings and communities and I feel great sympathy for the abolitionist movement (*Instead of Prisons*). However, I mistrust that without a social-economic-personal foundation on which to understand the function of the prison, abolitionist efforts, like all reform efforts, will become part and parcel of the prison strategies they are intended to correct. Without such a context abolition efforts will become essentially the same kind of activity as punishment.

To argue solely for abolishing prisons is comparable to arguing for taking obsolete bombers from the military. New warmaking machines are invented, new methods for selling the new machines are developed, methods that take into account and diminish the possibility of abolition in the future. It becomes an endless cycle in which human energies are fed into an inhuman furnace. The prohibition of alcoholic beverages brought greater and more intense drinking among Americans; greater sources of profit for distilling were available; and most importantly, there was greater police monitoring of a basic life function, the consumption of fluids. Similarly, abolition of slavery brought with it new forms of institutional racism, transforming the state itself into a new industrial plantation.

The more fundamental problem with abolition is that activities that attempt to obliterate or tear down do not bring of themselves any sense of community that endures or lead to living arrangements that can competently thrive without the state. They do not activate in people any deeper concern for everyday quality of life, for new tools of sociality or conviviality that foster social bonding in communities. While closing down can be swift, the development of tools for sociality is not and cannot be swift. To believe so is to embrace an illusion.

Abolitionists must face the importance of the symbolic function that the prison serves for the state. As the bald eagle is the symbol of America, the prison is the symbol of the state. The prison serves as a model for the perfected, utopian state, the panopticon state. The prison is a microcosm of the totalitarian state, where every aspect of life is treated as a commodity, where state officials have total control over the definition, means of expression, and satisfaction of human needs, the provision and rationing of supplies and materials for meeting those needs—supplies that state officials do not grow or process themselves but purchase with citizen taxes. As a structure, a process, a social context for living, the prison is the direct antithesis of the self-reliant community where individuals gain competency by doing things for themselves with others.

As social philosophers have visions of a perfect or just or free society that is characterized by freedom and solidarity among its members, state officials have visions of the state's perfected self, which microcosmically is reflected in the architecture and administration of the prison. The prison is a present miniature of a future complete state, the state come to its utopian fruition, the total societal institution, where the condition of the captives is not one of harmony with themselves, nature, and others but with the state as separated, commodity-ized individualities. In prison life processes are regulated from above, according to militaristic discipline; regimentation is both means and ends. It is a state of being in which there is only the absence of self, where all human presence is muffled and ultimately eliminated.

Abolitionists are correct in asserting that as long as the prison exists we are reminded that humankind is not in touch with the universe. Indeed, the prison is a sign that humankind is still attempting to master and enslave the universe, to capture its life and cage its variety to profitable proportions. It is also a sign that we are unnaturally situated in the universe. The prison, a container, a tool for those at odds with the state, is a machine of war, a political machine, a political statement that asserts all must be controlled or destroyed or disabled that we cannot understand. The prison is the perfect war machine, the perfect state in miniature, the antithesis to contemplation and mystical experience, when a person is at one with the universe. In prison a person is at two with nature, at two with him or herself. The prison is the machine that creates perfect schizo-existence.

What abolitionists must keep in mind is that the prison cannot, will not, be abolished as long as the state exists, for the prison is the state's map, the state's hope of its own utopia, the model that asserts that the perfect leviathan is a real possibility. The prisoners who dissented at Attica, for example, had to be mowed down by state officials, not simply because they threatened life themselves, but because they assaulted the model of the perfect state, the champion of the perfect state—publicly and collectively, through solidarity, the antithesis to state-defined living, to life as individualized, privatized existence. For the state to have allowed the dissenting prisoners to live would have been an open admission that collective action, action based on solidarity and mutual support, is more powerful than the individualizing state. It would have negated the thinking of panopticon ideology wherein "the crowd, a compact mass, a locus of multiple exchanges, individualities merging together, a collective effort, is abolished and replaced by a collection of separated individualities" (Bentham, 4:60–64).

While some readers might object that not enough has been written on the administration, social structure, and role arrangements in prisons for a treatise on corrections, I feel there is little value in such an exercise. The prison has no social value itself, only in relation to an exploitive system of production. What human value there might be in a more analytical or sociological approach to prison social structure is negated by the remarks of Hutchins Hapgood in an introduction to Alexander Berkman's prison memoirs, after Berkman had spent fourteen years doing hard time: "Prison life tends to destroy the body, weaken the mind and pervert the character. . . . Insanity is the natural result of prison life. It always tends to come" (Berkman, 1970).

14

TRIAGE ECONOMICS

New Realism Thinking

I mentioned earlier that most correctionalists by refusing to examine their assumptions about what they do have avoided a basic awareness of their relation to the state, an awareness of the state of their own personal unity. By denying the political-economic foundations of corrections, for example, many correctionalists historically have supported state ideology which attributes crime to personal pathology. By limiting themselves to asking; "What causes crime?" or "Who is a criminal?" or "Who is dangerous?" or "What kinds of punishment?" or "How long a confinement?" they continue to help mask the relationship between law and capitalist economics, between their own behavior and the social injustices they live among. The inference is always made, as Quinney remarks, that "the sources of crime are believed to be located in the person rather than in the authority that defines behavior as criminal. This emphasis has meant that criminal law and political theory have been ignored" (Quinney, 1974:13).

A cloak of mystery is allowed to rest around the vicious cycle of schisms created by capitalism as well as the vicious cycle of schisms created by one's own professional affiliations. It is among these schisms, their creation and mending, that one's questions as well as one's answers to questions of crime and punishment rest and often lay hidden. There is little, if any, appreciation of the fact that "crime, its meaning, extent, frequency, organization, and presence is one form of human misery," as Tifft asserts, or that, "the definition of crime is affected by and affects concomitants of justice, style of social control, and the structure of social relations" (1978:1-2).

In the meantime, with economics as a dimension excluded from their lives, correctionalists support a racist economy, a caste system which considers nature as something less than human and requiring conquest, which considers women to be inferior to men, children to be more reckless than adults, older people less useful than younger, darker-skinned people more dangerous than lighter-skinned, workers to be less responsible than managers, mutual aid to be less real than professional competence. The streets of communities that are potentially revolutionary are patrolled in a "preventive aggressive" fashion by professional safety specialists, and the people living in those inferiorized ghettos are bombarded with worthless conceptions of self, these conceptions themselves serving as a kind of ghetto. At the same time the streets of the elites are serviced in a "preventive passive" fashion. Correctionalists pursue drug traffic in the streets and homes of black and Hispanic neighborhoods for criminal conviction while other state-licensed professionals provide unlimited valium and librium prescription slips to relieve the anxiety, boredom, and depressions of people besieged by middle class schizo-existence. Professionals provide treatment for mothers who assault their children while male assailants are processed criminally. The two-track system applies to welfare assistance as well, where the poor are put through grueling and debasing ceremonies and rituals by unthinking and uncaring line workers while the corporate poor such as Rockwell, Boeing, Lockheed, and the oil cartels receive ongoing doses of economic stimulation in amounts that boggle the intelligence.

The changes that are occurring in capitalism now are important to understand, for they have implications of value for each of us, for the work each of us does. I am talking about an economy of new realism which requires new forms of human elimination and maintenance for political clientele, and loyalty from those who are to enforce the rules for these activities, political personnel. We now live in an era in which the cost of natural resources is going up and the value of human life is going down. The era is referred to euphemistically as one of slow economic growth. Technology has made an increasingly large number of people irrelevant to the production process. Mechanization and the centralization of the economies of the world "are drawing millions of people from subsistence farming into the international money economy in which they have no role as producer or consumer, for without jobs they do not have the money to buy food they once raised themselves" (Barnet, 33). Yet, "We are given the impression that there is growing criminality on the part of individuals and that this is inextricably related to the human search for a better material life or a more diverse cultural one" (Tifft, 1979). The changing state of multinational economics has created an international ideology of maintenance, or triage, a strategy of maintaining minimally "those who can be more productive and for consigning those who can't to various forms of 'benign neglect,' which for hundreds of millions means starvation" (Barnet, 33).

This new realism-triage thinking on an international level supports or justifies the multinational as an economic tool. This, in order to survive the slow growth era, must begin to devour its least aesthetic, least productive, least useful parts—the poor, the deviant, each of us who refuses to fit into the specifications of a maintenance-triage existence. It is important to understand the nature of this new realism internationally, for its domestic version has reared its head among us. Taking this multinational framework as a given, based on essentially a triage ethic, new realism correctionalists such as James Q. Wilson assert that "wicked people exist" and "nothing avails except to set them apart from innocent people."

The focus of correctionalists is more than ever on street crime, a political concept that means the political fallout of a racist economy. For the new realist, scientific cause-effect thinking is no longer useful, for in times of severe economic severity science is too indirect and too easily discredited by competing radical perspectives. The new realists gladly step from behind the mask of science and liberalism to argue the straightforward, state-based ideology that crime is race-specific (e.g., black people), place-specific (e.g., the streets), time-specific (e.g., night), manner-specific (e.g., predatory), and age-specific (e.g., the young). New realist thinking needs little to justify itself, for the justifications already exist, have been the backbone of penology and criminology for generations. It is a matter of reinforcing the prejudices people already have. New realism thinking, with its separatist foundations has parallel roots in the thinking that gave rise to the Nazi extermination ethic in the 1930s and that now supports and maintains the principle of apartheid in South Africa.

New realist thinking is not concerned with welfare but with totalizing, transporting the punitive—normalizing techniques that were developed and refined in the "helping game" directed to the entire social body, to every dimension of our lives. The authority we once saw limited to the sphere of judicial sentencing, for example, has now begun to infiltrate into "all other authorities that supervise, transform, correct, improve" (Foucault, 1977:303). In effect, the new realism state naturalizes the legal power to punish while at the same time it legalizes the technical power to discipline. This is the eventual outcome of rights-based theories, the application of the law by way of right to every aspect of our living together. The state becomes omnipresent, omnilegal, omninatural; all the administrative properties, acts, and intentions of the state are legal and humanly correct, and anything outside the state's domain is punishable as unhuman and unnatural. The state becomes the natural way to live! What is most astonishing about the study of corrections is that most people see its operations only in relation to "the criminal," a state abstraction, not in relation to acts of our collective lives. We have begun to accept the very machinery of the panopticon state in our everyday lives without being bothered by it—the most essential ingredient for a totalitarian living arrangement. Collective consciousness everywhere has been replaced by the separated individualities of Bentham's panopticon. We relate to each other through video machinery, alarms, and agents who register or monitor our behavior in supermarkets, libraries, clothing stores, food stores, banks, churches, bookstores, department stores, hospitals, elevators, workplaces. The American household turned residence has become a walled fortress with strident alarms and steel locks, barking dogs as signaling systems, armed residents who quell themselves to sleep with anxiety-reducing pills. Nearly every retail clerk in America today, anyone who does face-to-face business with people, is part of the panopticon's policing-detective system when he or she shares in the checking and monitoring of credit cards, packages, our persons, as we enter and leave stores. Our relationship to our supplies of food and clothing is one of militaristic disciplinization.

We all now live in a registered, quartered world. Birth, death, marriage, divorce, school, work, occupations are all registered, or else there is no legal access to them. Our very faults, our sins, our personal struggles, are registered as criminal, deviant, crazy, all reported in dossiers, our paper selves that move about quite apart from our natural bodies. Our medications are registered, our clergy are registered, our morticians, our teachers, our daycare centers, those who sell food, drink, clothing, books, those who sing to us!

We are already in the midst of the easeless state that Guibert foretold:

The state that I depict will have a simple, reliable, easily controlled administration. It will resemble those huge machines, which by quite uncomplicated means produce great effects; the strength of the state will spring from its own strength, its prosperity from its own prosperity. Time, which destroys all, will increase in power. It will disprove the vulgar prejudice by which we are made to imagine that empires are subjected to an imperious law of decline and ruin. [Foucault, 1977:169].

The society that Guibert speaks of is one in which all relationships are based on power and fixed social distance, rather than on free negotiation and mutual support. Self-regulation and self-determination are crushed beneath the state's urge toward the perfect hierarchy of life—the societal panopticon. Every human act requires permission of the state, creating a perverted version of the human person, for whom spontaneity is the essence of creativity. Liberty and freedom are disposed of as flights of fancy. State government is now prison government and prison government is now state government, in which freedom and time are excised from the person, as Lucas argues:

From then on, one can imagine the power of the education which, not only in a day, but in the succession of days and even years, may regulate for man the time of waking and sleeping, of activity and rest, the number and duration of meals, the quality and ration of food, the nature and product of labor, the time of prayer, the use of speech and even, so to speak that of thought, that education which, in the short, simple journeys from refectory to workshop, from workshop to the cell, regulates the movements of the body, and even in moments of rest, determines the use of time, the time-table, this education, which, in short, takes possession of man as a whole, of all the physical and moral faculties that are in him, and of the time in which he is himself. [Foucault, 1977:236]

I believe that time, that education, has already come upon us.

To divide people into wicked and innocent may be a tidy ideological tool that supports a particular political direction, but the division only serves to confuse our understanding of health and social unity, of life. This rationality of dichotomizing life is itself a symptom of the kind of insanity that applies to much of the human race today, especially the state and its professionals who keep trying to restore the insane and the wicked to the "real world" (Moran, 102).

If words like "sane/insane," "wicked/innocent," "knowing/ignorant" are to be considered valid to describe the human condition, they must apply along a continuum to every person, reflecting the totality of person. Those who characterize themselves as good or sane or innocent in an absolute fashion, exclude from the human, from themselves and others, what is in any way frightfully different, denying themselves any personal uniqueness and therefore a personal reality. This thinking makes any alternate reality, though it may mean the expression and presence of more of the human self, a truth too painful to bear, and therefore an unreality. For each person who is sane/insane, good/evil, there is a risk of being singled out for attempting to be all that one is, human. What we need to do is enlarge our concept of the human so that it includes all that appears. As human beings we can no longer afford to limit ourselves to political, megamachine definitions of life. If we refuse to accept our sick and insane parts, the daimonic in ourselves, as part of the human, and a necessary part of health, the sane, mutual supporting aspects of ourselves will continue to elude us. We will become more solidified in the robopathic, totalitarian economy that continues to creep into our humanity daily.

III

REEXAMINING THE FOUNDATIONS FOR SAFETY

Person, Punishment, Power

THE CHILD IN MAN

Innocence is in the time of child
When wonderment comes—even in a fly.
Who and What and Where and Why
Crowds every moment of the fertile field.

Somehow, the child changes; days go by,
The child, in man to be caricature.
Impoverished, indebted, unable, impure;
The golden years of innocence so swiftly die.

Forget man's dreams and schemes—so wild.
A better man comes not with gain and treasure.
They better live who increase the mind's measure
And share, in love for all—less man, more the child.

Richard Rudolph

15

PERSON

The Foundation for Unity

Social integration or social unity takes place only as each person becomes integrated within him or herself. Any work concerned with fostering community safety or social unity therefore, must take into account at some point current images of person, the self in society. These images or conceptions of person tend to serve as boundaries or upper limits to what is admissible within experience, within our everyday relationships. Based on the images of self created, a society builds its social tools as well as renders judgments about the nature and degree of control necessary for fostering human experience, social harmony and quality of life. A major premise of this book is that the social tools currently in use in our culture are counterproductive to both personal and social unity, for they are based on assumptions about person geared not to satisfy the needs or well being of all but of groups of economic and expertise elites.

The folly of most correctionalists writing today is to dismiss the relevancy of any discussion about person from their understanding or to make the issues about person a matter of sides, the choice being between whether people are essentially good or wicked, angel or beast at their core. More often than not, when person is considered, it is usually the self as an isolated entity, so that any social analysis tends to break down. When the self is examined apart from its organic context, there is no way out to the social setting in which that self struggles for meaning, for authenticity. Particularly in this decade of "meism" and self-awareness, understanding of the relational nature of person is often avoided or its importance denied. But so also is the possibility of understanding the social conditions that influence the self to act in different ways, for example, by power or free agreement. I believe that most social scientists have seen the social darwinist, survival of the fittest principle as the only social context for understanding relationship, and having despaired of other possibilities for creating community, have minimized the importance of sociality for evolution.

From the outset I must emphasize that our understanding of person here is relational, that is, it "is a bringing to light the presence of being *among men. Understanding is always of people together* in a world" (Moran, 94). Social unity is a particular way of relating, a particular qualitative way of relating. It is essential therefore to have some sense of not only what this way or means of relationship is, but some sense of the current image of person as that which relates. The current work of correctionalists who have chosen to examine the issues around person, even those who consider themselves revolutionary, is of little help in understanding person, for they have worked within the same models used for centuries. It is a notion of person, which Kropotkin for one illustrated with great patience, based on extremely limited information about the opposing factors of power and cooperation in primitive peoples (1934:62–83).

When there have been changes in the definition of person, the changes have generally occurred in a pendulum fashion. When people seem to get out of hand (e.g., after the nineteen-sixties of this century, after the revolutions in England and France), there is a tightening of institutional control and concepts of person are modified to point a finger at the lingering beast in man. When things seem to settle down, the institutional belt is let out a notch or two, and the concept of person as bestial is modified to include some additional bits of the angelic.

This has been the recurring history of sociology. Rather than reexamining the social context in which human hurts and social harms occur, to discover those elements that support breakdown in connectedness or interrelationship, sociologists historically have simply pointed to the dark recesses of the human soul. Sometimes they have done this indirectly, for example, by withdrawing from the struggling community and justifying their acts with such rationales as scientific objectivity, or value-free method, neutrality, etc. They then could watch the community and provide rationales for its behavior by equating watching with sharing or sympathy.

But the history of humankind, and the daily resolution of conflicts and differences in our own lives, disallows such a simplistic view. Relationship, the nature of people, the needs and awareness of those involved in relationship, are considerably more complex. If the human person is in some way torn, struggling with opposing forces within, it makes little sense to avoid this fact by taking sides, claiming that people are stupid or evil or crazy by nature. It is precisely this taking of sides that has made corrections and theories of change a battle of wills over which side is right, an enforcement of justifications for a quick and decisive victory for one's side, so that then all can get down to the practical business of correcting. This approach leads not to new consciousness but to battered, defensive spirits, most often resulting in one's immovable position along an imaginary ideology line of political radical/conservative.

At the same time a person denies his or her own authenticity. This is the status of work being done on justice today as people separate further into left and right positions, in which there is increasingly less room for openly expressed doubt about one's position in life, little room to question one's humanity, little room for uncertainty. To be practical, as the avowed pragmatists would have it, the result is inevitably relationship treated as a political-economic commodity, as a thing to be produced by one group, consumed by another. For example, the task of the left is to get the right to assume its particular brand of ideology. What is not taken into account is that the positions people take on political lines are often frustrated attempts to express their own different and unique personal needs. Questions of existence, being, and quality of life are sacrificed for some strange sense of needing a firm political position. This is the insanity we are confronted with today, and it seems to me the greatest problem of corrections. It seems that "only by continually raising the question of being or to be (as distinct from questions about beings) can man remain in contact with his true self and what is real" (Moran, 93). But it is exactly this kind of context, that of being, which is shouted down as irrelevant, impractical, and dreamy, which suggests that what is thought to be practical today is not the most sane course to take.

The hierarchical ordering of persons in a society into wicked/innocent by the new realists is a good example of the taking sides approach I have been talking about. This ordering of groups or persons, or for that matter societies, comes from the insistence of economists that the progress of the human person—as industrialist or corporationalist—is the measure of all things. The world of raw materials (including people themselves) is viewed as only a means, as something to be transformed and then consumed for the sake of progress or the evolution of species. In our present culture even the natural elements are not understood in their own right, as Hannah Arendt once predicted: "The wind will no longer be understood in its own right as a natural force but will be considered exclusively in accordance with human needs. . . ."

The difficulty with the kind of thinking, or more accurately, way of life, that Arendt criticized is that it tends to equate the use that technology makes of any part of nature (persons, materials, the elements, etc.)

with the whole meaning of the thing and to view the nature of persons and materials in accord with technological requirements. The positive value or goodness of a thing or being—the world, people, relationship, existence—is judged solely in terms of its potential for output, production, marketability, profit-margins, etc. This has brought us to a social existence of strangers, to treatment of each other as objects, processible raw materials. It is this kind of thinking that has brought us to our present state of what I believe to be a cold civil war, a form of social suicide, a condition Mumford foresaw as inevitable for a consumption economy: "For man to restrict his social activities and his personal fulfillments solely to those that conform to external megatechnic requirements would be a form of collective suicide: and that suicide—or more accurately biocide—is in fact taking place before our eyes" (1970:384).

There are many people who distrust using our present relations in community as a starting point, arguing that a more solid foundation is necessary to make sense of the complex social problems in our society. But I maintain that these relations are the most solid and fundamental foundation there is and that we must look to their mutually supportive aspects as the foundation for human experience and hence justice. No limits are to be set either at the beginning or the end for what might somehow be in, with, or under the mutual aid we can provide for each other. Without such a starting point, there can be no sense of justice or morality, for mutual aid-justice-morality are consecutive steps in an ascending series. Any other starting point negates coming to grips with any sense of justice, for it avoids coming to grips with recurring human needs.

In developing theories of correcting, correctionalists by rejecting our relationship with each other as a starting point limit themselves to definitions of person that are based on the hierarchical, competitive principles evident in capitalism. In trying to make sense of human relationship, correctionalists have limited themselves to the thinking of one particular set of economic principles that time and time again disprove their ability to confirm or enhance human experience. The view of person most often taken reflects an economy of self contained in the Freudian dictum "All that has been id shall be ego." This means that only that which is transformable is good, has value. While this view of person as a composite of conscious/unconscious elements might have been a helpful beginning for scientists leaving behind the old and frail theological body-spirit split, the way scientists approached the unconscious and the reasons they delved into it, created another split, another hierarchical ordering of self. It is this hierarchical ordering that has helped to reinforce our thinking of the human person as an untrustworthy creature. One can hardly hope to begin living cooperatively with that which is feared most, namely, each other.

Though Freud's dictum, which served as a reinforcement for all modern political theories of crime and punishment such as that of Hobbes, a value judgment is placed on the unconscious as *less than* the conscious, requiring control or management, "a governing power which creates morality under fear of punishment." As far as human experience or experiencing humanly is concerned, the only value of the unconscious is utilitarian, for what it might be in the future. The unconscious is seen as something to be transformed into the mainstream of self, the conscious ego. The mistake here is to suppose that the newly discovered unconscious is the bad part of self, to be controlled or eliminated or more correctly transformed as much as possible. That would produce safety and allow fears to reside. From this kind of thinking one gets the sense that the basic drive of the human person is always toward self-destruction, away from sociality and mutually supportive relationships. Of course, the irony is that we are a culture with the most pervasive state in history, with one of the most fear-ridden peoples in history, if the number of books and television talk shows produced on the subject is any accurate indicator of the range and depth of human fear.

Given this framework, the self-reliant, autonomous, free person is little more than some underside of self brought into the light, brought under the control of the rational, watchful self socialized by the protective institutions of the watchful state. Only a completed self or a completed community has value, not the unfinished, struggling, mysterious self. The major problem of course is that there is never positive human value in the present. There is only future value, when something is complete, when someone is finished or whole, retired or dead, none in the means or process getting there. Those who tend to isolate the self in this dichotomized fashion of finished/unfinished, innocent/wicked, tend to spend their lives looking over their shoulders for the possible uncontrollable expression of the beast in others, simultaneously keeping strict guard over their own selves lest their own inner beasts make public appearance and unleash themselves upon others. As far as human relationships are concerned, one always has to be on guard, in control, for intimacy is not safe, safety is not intimate.

It is this kind of thinking about the nature of people, in essentially industrial or production terms, that brought children to be viewed as a special category of human being—the underside of the adult world. The child in our present society is still treated "as a distinctive social category: children have their own special psychology, their own special needs, patterned processes of growth often elaborated into ideas about developmental stages which may postpone advent to (full) adulthood well into a person's twenties, and sometimes still later." (Berger, 10–12). The specialized, graded education system, the juvenile court, are tools which those in authority attempt to use for socializing the beast at its most un-controllable but seemingly malleable stage. Children are raised or produced (do not grow up) according to scientifically elaborated principles of proper child management—"a process which in many families results in the dif-ferentiation of family roles in a way that transforms a woman with child into a full-time child raiser" (Jerome, 216). And historically the woman was the child raiser for, comparatively, she was regarded as less bestial or less beast-ridden than her male partner. The wife-female partner in essence becomes an employee for the husband-male partner, both of whom treat child rearing as containment. Regardless of role, however, it is supposed that all have to be watched.

Once again, scientific thinking about person reinforced this thinking. While Freud had a great respect for the mind, he nevertheless saw it as "No peacefully contained unity. It is rather to be compared with a modern state in which a mob, eager for enjoyment and destruction, has to be held down forcibly by a prudent superior class" (1963:303), namely, Freud and his colleagues, who can deliver to this uncontrollable mass what will keep it in bounds. This view does not differ significantly from the sentiments of Moynihan quoted earlier, where the poor had to be monitored if they were to become a part of the upperside of society, and yet perhaps they might never become a part. It might be called a social darwinist position, whereby only the fittest, the most astute, sur-vive. Huxley described the situation as follows:

The weakest and stupidest went to the wall, while the toughest and shrewd-est, those who were best fitted to cope with their circumstances, but not the best in another way, survived. Life was a continuous free fight, and beyond the limited and temporary relations of the family, the Hobbesian war of each against all was the normal state of existence.

The possibility of free and autonomous communities has been under-mined by this same kind of thinking, for groups of people, neighborhoods only aggravate exponentially what exists in the daimonic individual. Communities can not be guided by cooperation, for they are bound by the same "inexorable principle" that Freud saw in the individual. The group, he insisted is "an obedient herd, which could never live without a master. It has such a thirst for obedience that it submits instinctively to anyone who appoints himself as its master" (1948:15-21). For correc-tionalists, such conceptions of self and the group have served as the under-lying rationale for dividing people into good and bad, into the beastlike and the pure of heart. Similarly, these conceptions have served as subtle justifications for maintaining ghettos as the visible just deserts of the impure inner selves of their inhabitants.

The objectivity of scientific method, which has its roots in the same political economy as this view of person and group has, only served to reinforce social divisions. Scientists, for example, claimed that too great a proximity to the bestial proportions of a person or group confounds a rational approach to experience. The person, the group, must be observed from afar. Equally importantly, objectivity also provides a form of personal safety for the scientific observer. On the one hand, it permits the observer to oversee human affairs from afar, always as a matter of scientific curiosity and design, rather than as a search for personal meaning. The relational distance from one's subjects (a euphemism for objects) also saves him or her from ever having to encounter the frightening possibility of coming face-to-face with an alternate reality in others. On the other hand, the scientist, by living according to the principles of method, never has to face the possibility that the source of that alternate reality he or she fears out there might reside somewhere within him or herself. Subjective involvement of one's person in one's work, the expression of one's innermost needs for cooperation and immersion in community, is ruled out on grounds of scientific purity. It would only produce "corrupted" sociology, when in fact the reason is the very human fear of taking the personal risk that one's inner self might contain the very demons that one's outer professional self has spent all kinds of funding money, a professional lifetime, trying to cleanse from others. The scientist would be no different from the rest of humankind and would be faced with living on equal footing with others in confronting human misery.

In an attempt to establish a theory of justice, Rawls follows the same kind of ordering of person I have been talking about, which always provides as a corollary, the state. The state is seen as "an organ for guaranteeing that self-interested individuals do not let their self-interest destroy the compact of cooperation" (61). Rawls's point of view stems from the same set of formulations offered by the Italian criminologist Caesare Beccaria a century and a half earlier. Beccaria had argued in his *On Crimes and Punishment* that people "weary of living in a continual state of war, and of enjoying a liberty which became of little value, from the uncertainty of its duration, . . . sacrificed one part of it, to enjoy the rest in peace and security." Even current theorists who propose revolutionary platforms fall into the same error about person, always having "the inferior" kept beneath the tutelage of "the superior"; human consciousness is not created by encouraging people to be free but to submit to tutelage. Quinney quotes Hill in this regard: "While there are many negative tendencies among the lumpen, their hatred of the system and courage in fighting it should not be ignored. If led by a strong and disciplined proletarian revolutionary movement, elements of the lumpen can become courageous allies of the working class" (86–87). There is little recognition on the part of most marxists writing today that class analysis as a starting point creates an inevitable schism, one that always leads away from "the species-essence" that Karl Marx looked for but which always eluded him. Class analysis leads to a revolution which creates new, more encompassing forms of ownership, those of the state.

Correctionalists are consistent but mistaken in arguing for tools that check or regulate the self-interest aspects of people, when it is this very act of checking or guaranteeing on the part of the state and its helping professions that keeps people from becoming authentic. Contrary to what most people believe it is the self-interest in people, when allowed to exist in its fullest proportions, that brings forth the need or instinct for mutuality and cooperation, that is the foundation for human experience. The theories that we have inherited from Hobbes, Beccaria, Rawls, Wilson, and even Quinney, among others, are so concerned with getting to a just society that they lose getting at the full range of the human person, the dimensions that enable us to survive cooperatively. One might suppose that they are not as desirous to experience life or to foster human experience. As is often thought, it may be safer to use one's head all the time in the production of political solutions than to let experience flow in and out of one's being. Historically, we see that

individual liberty, freedom and self autonomy are lost to the collective totality (the state) which allocates equity, primary goods (liberty, opportunity, income, wealth, base of self respect), identity and life itself. Why can't we recognize that liberty and opportunity for the individual are found in inverse ration to the power of the state? Why can't we see that human misery cannot be reduced or eliminated through institutional modes, themselves inherently productive of misery? [Tifft and Sullivan, 1977:6–7].

The mistake that people make in accepting scientific objectivity in these matters is that it does not reflect a neutral or value-free position but an abstracted position. Therefore models of justice and correction based on objectivity are not grounded in human experience. They reflect a strong "alienation from self and society, it is alienation from a society experienced as a hurtful and unloving thing. Objectivity is the way one comes to terms and makes peace with a world one does not like and will not oppose" (Gouldner, 103). These models reflect a strong self-interest but one that is denied. The very life of Hobbes, for one, makes this clear. His pervasive disgust with political revolution in England brought him to view the political struggle with fervor, but at a distance. His *Leviathan* expounded a way to live in a cruel world but one in which he could be buffered from the conflicts.

It should be clear how scientific objectivity and professional expertise are linked to a state-directed, capital-intensive economy. All rule out human needs as the foundation for living together. A needs-based economy, based on the subjective assessment of each person's needs, is seen as ridiculous, for there always resides in the objective viewer the untested fear that one's own person may be the entity that will get out of control, that will be the greedy and beastlike person feared all along. And worse, this isolated person in need may require the support of persons who have been judged daimonic and unrewarding, oozing with demons of greed (that one has sought to exterminate in others) just waiting for the first opportunity to be unleashed upon the needy, vulnerable spirit. Being free, for the objectifying person, is never a real possibility, because it is never a present possibility or a possibility of shared presence, for the self is always tucked neatly away in some corner of an updated method geared to explain the mystery that confounds one's mind.

Clearly, there are unknown, mysterious, and often frightening dark sides to the human person that sometimes envelop the experiencing person. This always seems to be the case where there is some potential for human growth and creativity. I maintain that it is not possible to unify a society that we divide into wicked and innocent unless we first look at the wicked/innocent struggle in ourselves. The first step is to recognize that such a struggle exists in each of us in pretty much the same way, the second that this struggle cannot be experienced *as it is* through a lifestyle of objective analysis or professional expertise. Only by facing and personally experiencing what is recognized as "other" in ourselves, seeing that "other" as valuable for what it is, not for what it might be, and including all that appears as comprising the human will, do we begin to face humanly what is "other" in society—be it wicked, insane, deviant, or harmful. Dreams, magic mystery, madness and hurts have as much claim on reality as the objective world that demands their conformity to some grand, absolute vision of a correct life.

To begin to face the totality of our whole person is not without its anguish, as the existentialists have noted (Blackham). It is, however, a move away from the desperate quietism and confusion that correctionalists find themselves presently enveloped in, not a helpless immersion in it. Sidney Jourard writes of a person's coming to face this kind of holistic experience:

This hidden dimension of self, sought for centuries by men who have longed for personal fulfillment beyond rationalism, is usually dreaded by the average person. It could be called "experiencing possibility." It sometimes peeps out when one permits himself to be unfocused and aimless, unintegrated, not going anywhere or doing anything; but it is "tamped back" in anxious haste, for it is experienced like the contents of Pandora's box. [Jourard, 45]

There is no social reality, no hope for personal and social unity, except through this kind of action, through "experiencing possibility" in ourselves. It is only then that each of us can begin to understand the dichotomies we project upon others, their utter meaninglessness. Human experience is living in search for unity through possibility. All else is "miscarried hopes" (Sartre, 33).

The difficulty with most of our modern history concerned about personal awareness is that by hierarchically ordering person for safeness, we have prevented ourselves from seeing the human person as he or she is—*neither beast nor angel but human,* a composite of both. We have not been willing to take the risk to peek into Pandora's box, head on. History also tends to minimize or trivialize the unconscious as an entity in itself, instead of reflecting an openness to the human possibilities that pervade the unconscious. Norman Brown is an exception, showing great sensitivity to the unconscious as a reality that has worth in itself:

The unconscious, then, is not a closet full of skeletons in the private house of the individual mind; it is not even, finally, a cave full of dreams and ghosts in which like Plato's prisoners, most of us spend most of our lives. The unconscious is rather the immortal sea which brought us hither; intimations of which are given in moments of "oceanic feeling"; one sea of energy or instinct, embracing all mankind, without distinction of race, language, or culture; and embracing all the generations of Adam, past, present, and future, in one phylogenetic heritage; in one mystical or symbolic body. [Brown, 88–89]

The unconscious is complete in itself. It is the material by which we are bound to each other in our naked humanity, free of the boundaries and illusions of imposed, profit-based realities. It is through the movement and presence of the unconscious that each of us begins to recognize his or her uniqueness, the freedom of his or her own choices, choices which are deeply personal but which also include all humankind. In responding to the incessant flow of possibility that exists within each of us, we create an image of the world as we think it ought to be, we create our dreams of the perfect self, the ideal in which we begin to find meaning for ourselves, both individually and collectively (Brown, 17).

In this conception of self or person, the unconscious and conscious are not hierarchically ordered parts of self, with a pervasive lid of sanity covering the top of the unconscious, but interdependent. We see that the unconscious and conscious grow together and that each is dependent upon the other for fostering personal definition and self-awareness. To repress one of these dimensions by considering it intrinsically less than the other is to repress all the creative aspects of self, as well as deny the human tendency toward sociality, self-regulation, and self-enhancement. Both conscious and unconscious must be seen as interdependent parts of a whole and "as the islands of the conscious grow broader the surrounding seas of the unconscious grow deeper" (Bellah, 206) and the experiencing person becomes more fully human, not less so. A person can begin to become, as Kierkegaard notes, "that self which one truly is" (29). Clearly, if we wish to begin to understand the delicate interplay between the conscious and unconscious of those who hurt themselves and others, we cannot continue to rely on the impersonal acts of the state correctional complex.

As most people writing about relationship today would have it, the unconscious, the daimonic, is not the destructive elements in a person but the urge to be free and interdependent simultaneously, as Rollo May asserts: "The daimonic is the urge in every being to affirm itself, assert itself, perpetuate and increase itself." It may be that part of self, May continues, that "skates on the edge of exploitation of the partner (the other); but without it, there is no vital relationship" (146), no unity or wholeness. In the tradition of Rilke, if we are to have our angels, we must also have our devils! If both are to exist as they are, an essential part of growth, will require the support of others, for human fulfillment can be found only in the mutual support of each other's struggle to be more human. Mutual aid or mutual support is as much a part of the history of human community as the Hobbesian war of each against all, so the required support I am talking about is not without precedent. The expression or presence of one or the other aspects of self, angels or devils, is dependent upon the social conditions in which we choose to live, namely, cooperatively or competitively.

Carl Rogers discovered the importance of social conditions for personal growth decades ago in his practice of psychotherapy (1970). He found that all a therapist could really do was to form a mutual alliance with another person, to be attentive, receptive to the total, experiencing person before him. Healing was not a matter of providing a service or of having something like old personal baggage transferred from the troubled person to the therapist. Nor was the key to human growth or well being, which Rogers repeatedly discovered, in any form of regulation of the suffering person but pure and simple receptivity to all that the person was experiencing. Only under the conditions of mutual support would people begin to experience their whole selves. Not only were they able to discover their own uniqueness, they began to discover the necessity of mutual support for maintaining their uniqueness among others. Through mutual aid a person can begin to discover with all the intensity of his or her being that there is something of great worth to be reckoned with, his or her own existence.

In a therapeutic context Rogers had discovered what Kropotkin had observed in social groups, namely, the necessity of mutual aid as a factor in evolution, as a factor in personal and social progress. Kropotkin noted that mutual aid "most probably has a far greater importance (than mutual struggle), inasmuch as it favours the development of such habits and characters as insure the maintenance and further development of the species, together with the greatest amount of welfare and enjoyment of life for the individual, with the least waste of energy" (1902:6). As Kropotkin had been ostracized for his social beliefs that emerged from his study of mutual aid, Rogers had also been warned by the Menninger Clinic in 1951 about his method, for possibly being conducive to unleashing madness upon the rest of the world. Rather, the opposite has been the case, namely, that as people are encouraged to experience themselves fully, as they begin to disclose themselves to each other, they begin to see themselves as trustworthy; they begin to see that their basic nature is not something to be feared or denied or given over to an imposing, waiting Leviathan but can unfold and release energies in a responsible fashion. In short, people begin to behave and experience humanly when they trust the support of others to be authentic and the social concerns of others to be authentic concerns for community.

16

PUNISHMENT AND HUMAN EXPERIENCE

If social integration can occur only as people become integrated within themselves, it is important to have a deeper understanding of the social conditions under which people are encouraged to grow up and mature, to recover from difficulties, to become whole and self-reliant. The nature of the social conditions within each cultural context fosters and gives meaning to specific interpersonal relations, in particular how benefits and burdens are to be shared in. The social, political, economic context of life that a person accepts as real and meaningful influences his or her sense of responsibility for him or herself and others. One's view of self and relationship both shapes and is shaped by one's everyday social world. An understanding of society is simply a bringing to light the fact that "each person is unique, diverse, physically and existentially separate" (Tifft, 1978:1). The paradox is that the discovery of this uniqueness is thwarted, becomes elusive and illusory, unless we are united in each other's need to search for and create meaning. A person's search for community is his or her search for uniqueness and meaning, and vice versa, and the more conscious one is of being bound to others and to nature, the freer one is to be one's unique, different, and autonomous self.

Given the fact that our view of person and society is relational, one wonders about the narrow, one-dimensional approach correctionalists have taken historically to understand hurts and social harms. In their support of the state and competitive, power-based economic system as a means to heal, they show little understanding that it is under these social conditions that violence, greed, and exploitation have become a way of life. They support and argue in behalf of the very conditions that lead to social decay and continued isolated existence for individuals. Open any page of correctional literature and you will find it expressed either directly or by way of assumption that only through the state can individuals find human solidarity! Correctionalists reinforce the position of the state that not only is it possible to secure compliance from people through punishment, and thereby reduce the "amount" of harm that exists in a community, but that punishment is the only tool or means toward safety or harmony. Whether in arguments over the value of capital punishment, longer or shorter sentences, determinate or indeterminate sentences, state-based ideology has it that punishment protects, punishment deters, punishment works as a means toward personal and social integration. Through punishment individual uniqueness is insured and human meaning attained.

Most correctionalists, for example, would have us believe that the historical variations in punishment strategies or justifications (e.g., deterrence, retribution, rehabilitation, just deserts) reflect changing human concerns, attempts on the part of the state to adapt to the increasing complexity of the modern era. The reality is: a capitalist industrial complex responds internally to changing economic conditions, shifting its illusion-generating power from this fashion in the mask of love to that, so as to justify its own economic and symbolic worth in a utilitarian economic order. The age of reform, the invention of the penitentiary, the introduction of probation and parole as administrative concepts, support this economic view to a penny. The prison system, what we might describe as the whole correctional experience, is antithetical to what we know about people, how people change and grow, how they fail and recuperate. The prison, the state complex, is a sign of disregard for the facts about our humanity. Punishment is a misreading of our humanity; it shows ignorance of what it means to be human and struggling to be free and whole.

Punishment destroys freedom and wholeness, for it destroys the possibilities of our being bound to each other. With their foundations in fear and power, human encounters are seen as win-lose situations in which conflicts are zero-sum, one claim superior (the state's) the other inferior (the individual's or the community's). With punishment as a means, there is never the possibility to become integrated, to be that self which one truly is, for there is never the conciliatory new consciousness that one is in any way connected. People are forced through hierarchical relationships either to live in the past, to recapture past losses, or to skip to some place in the future and hang on to some revolutionary dream. Either way there is a withdrawal from present reality, from the struggle to connect with others in the present.

Even when correctionalists have introduced humane-sounding justifications for their punishing activities under the auspices of individualized treatment or now just deserts, the reality has always been the same. It turns out to be more of the same battering punishment, cloaked beneath more refined official garments. It is always a device for breaking a person's will to resist, "hounding him into compliance with institutional demands, and is thus a means to exerting maximum control. The cure will be deemed effective to the degree that the poor or young or brown or black captive appears to have capitulated to the middle class or white or middle-aged captor, and to have adopted the virtues of subservience to authority, industry, cleanliness, docility" (Mitford, 116–117). Although Jessica Mitford is talking about relationship in the prison, the same social conditions are experienced in schools, families, the workplace, and medicine today where relationship is thought of in terms of commodity. The function of these institutions is to foster not self-reliant people and autonomous communities but a particular type of economic being, the docile consumer.

17

PUNISHMENT FACTS

To justify the maintenance and continuing expansion of the state punishment complex, correctionalists have maintained an allegiance to science, shifting their justifications from the criminal act to the criminal, then back again to the criminal act. What correctionalists, who view life processes in a pendulum fashion, fail to recognize is that the problem with punishment is not what form the justifications take but that relationship leading to human experience requires justification at all. Moreover, they seem to omit the fact that no matter what justification is selected, hierarchical, power-based relationships are created and maintained which are essentially destructive to the human spirit. Nevertheless, the history of corrections and penology continues to be an endless parading of new punishment forms, exhibited before an impatient public, selected with the depth and feeling of winning bingo numbers.

As government and private funding agency monies have flowed into the pockets of correctionalists, into their agencies and universities through indirect costs, they have searched for the core of the criminal, that core place within a person where they might apply the doses of scientifically prepared and state-certified punishment. Correctionalists have descended upon the correctional client like a hawk, peering into his or her chromosomes, intelligence level, skull shape, tattoos, sexual habits, work habits, speech patterns, clothing design, and writing styles. They have scaled prisoner perception of time, of authority, of self, over time and under different authorities. The roles he or she assumed during imprisonment were charted, their relationships with all kinds of prison staff were studied methodically, with guards, fellow prisoners, cottage parents, therapists, counselors, teachers, lawyers, even the researchers themselves. There was no sign of human growth or personal wholeness from the punishment methods.

Various types of sentences were introduced. Longer sentences were tried, then shorter sentences; then longer sentences were reintroduced. Determinate sentences were changed to indeterminate sentences, then back again to determinate sentences. Fines were introduced, then fines with jail, probation plus a fine, probation plus jail, parole, then parole revocation. The result was the same—no sign of human growth or personal wholeness with punishment.

Prisoners were placed in halfway houses, in group homes, on parole or work release, off parole. They were persuaded to live according to the principles of token economies, aversive therapies, psychotherapy, psychodrama, psychosurgery, reality therapy. The effects were weighed and reweighed with the latest statistical tools, but to no avail when it came to human experience or competency to live cooperatively among others.

Prisoners have been put under varying degrees of supervision in special cottages, special tiers, given special food to eat, special books to read, special medicines. Collegefields, Essexfields, Highfields—all kinds of fields treatment have been given. Prisoners have been put into maximum, medium, minimum, maximum-maximum, and solitary confinement quarters. They have been forced to live under various degrees of deprivation of sound, touch, and light. Their behavior has been recorded microscopically, like bacteria on a laboratory slide. Deprivation upon deprivation has been imposed and its effects studied and analyzed. The data are subject to rigorous analyses by graduate students and stored in increasingly larger computers for dissertations on punishment. The name of the place of confinement is changed from "penitentiary" to "correctional institution," "facility," "center," even "home." The prisoner is given new titles as a way to increase self worth such as "inmate," "ward," "patient," "resident," "citizen," and "student." The effects of these changed conditions have been measured and remeasured but as far as human experience goes, to no avail. There is no sign of human growth, no sign of community among those on whom the state's endless benefits are bestowed.

The list is endless. New forms of status, new communication arrangements, new managerial styles, new forms of managed cooperation, new identities, new skills, new bodies, new minds, plans, programs, thoughts, contracts, privileges, tokens—and still the experience of the whole correctional system remains an inhuman experience, showing no signs of human growth or the growth of community based on warmth and caring.

If one examines the activities of the American correctional system from its inception, we see that the state has never had a positive influence in reducing hurtful behavior for, as I have emphasized throughout, it takes away the very aspects of persons that bring them closer together. Epidemics of crime have come and gone, without any demonstrable impact on the part of the state. From the colonial period on official wars have been waged with stocks gallows, fines and whips, public and private shamings, prisons, therapies, beatings, killings, rifles, teargas, drugs, lethal injection, and psychosurgery. Computers, businesslike management strategies, college-educated personnel, have been introduced as supports for the ever-new technological hardware, yet there is no evidence or sign of human growth or community-based competency. In fact, the opposite is true, we witness daily a steady deterioration in community as the state increases its repertoire of illusions about its effectiveness. Even the new, freshly educated personnel introduced by state officials as organizational window dressing burn out at a quicker rate than ever. Crime and harm seem to ebb and flow according to changes in the economic conditions of society and to the extent to which people's needs are being met directly by themselves or are being turned into profit-inducing commodities (Rusche and Kirchheimer).

Finally, if anyone can speak of an organic way to live, correctional officialdom in every aspect contradicts this condition. In instances where human concerns have been shown by correctional personnel and received by their clients, they have had to disown their affiliation with the state-professional complex and involve themselves in the life of the community or those they help. The Catholic Worker Movement in America is a good example of this. (Day) Those who work as part of the state are distrusted for the state's needs always take precedence. Those correctionalists who come with the hope that accompanies innovation are quickly disillusioned and cast into despair. Even the redone setting of an old red barn is to no avail to counteract the poisonous effects of the system, as Nagel notes:

The institutions were new and shiny, yet in all their finery they still seemed to harden everyone in them. Warm people enter the system wanting desperately to change it, but the problems they find are so enormous and the tasks so insurmountable that these warm people turn cold. In time they can no longer allow themselves to feel, to love, to care. To survive, they must become callous. The prison experience is corrosive for those who guard and those who are guarded. [148]

It is not possible to claim one's humanity and consider oneself part of the human community if one finds meaning in punishment, as Pat McAnany has noted: "It is the struggle with the meaninglessness of punishment in our present context that pushes us toward justice beyond the law courts. It does make sense, though it might not be totally explainable, that a man 'pay' for his crime. *But it will only make sense when there is a moral universe within which we all operate.*" How can anyone continue to live by and support punishment-based acts, given the history of punishment, namely, that wherever it has reared its head, people and communities begin to disintegrate.

18

PUNISHMENT AND EXPERIENCE

A Matter of Presence

It is possible to contradict these facts on punishment as most correctionalists seem to do or at least tend to avoid them, and argue that punishment as a means of correcting may not work, but that it is because of existing administrative conditions such as insufficient budget allowances, insufficient personnel, lack of public support, lack of educated or well-prepared personnel. This is in fact what the classic liberal has continued to assert throughout his or her lifetime, providing an endless procession of change agent roles for themselves, by which they can purify state agencies or state clientele through management. This is essentially the thinking of the superprofessional, namely, that punishment will work with the correct admixture of advanced management. As I did earlier with the more specific notion of rehabilitation, I would like to discuss the underlying philosophical foundations of punishment in relation to human experience and to show that punishment as a means to human experience, whether we call it learning or working or healing, is an impossibility, for it destroys the essence or means of experience, human presence.

Human experience, human growth, and deeply personal relationships cannot emerge without one's presence, without the present expression of one's being. As Martin Buber stated, "I become through my relation to the *Thou*, as I become I, I say *Thou*" (1958:11). And vice versa, as each "thou" is spoken, the conditions for me to become myself are created, so that I repeat my "thou" once again. Human relationship, at a minimum, suggests an exchange that moves toward the full engagement and expression of both parties. This does not mean that both parties must be or are equal in every respect, but there must be some foundation of equality, a common ground of experience from which both might express themselves, might experience together, and thus be present to each other. This common ground constitutes the human need, the well being of each.

Therefore the quality of presence, of being present, as I am using the term here, means more than "I am here." It carries with it a deep sense of one's own personage as viable and sharing, containing an element of collectivity or universality. By being present to another, I am present to all and can affirm: "I am here, in this place, with these beings. I am part of history." It is through such an experience of self and others that I develop an awareness of self as creator of what is and what might be. I can begin to move beyond the immediacy of the here and now and take possession of my past and create a future of meaning for myself. Human presence allows a person to transcend what is presently binding and to find meaning in pursuing his or her dreams, for a person's dreams have their grounding in present relationship. The more genuine or real the relationship—the more each partner gives and receives freely—the more each partner can abandon absolutes, fixed points, and a priori abstractions as prerequisites for experiencing.

Presence frees a person from having, from owning, from privatizing, so as *to be now* and also to have a future (a new past, so to speak), for one's past need not be escaped from. Without this present of meaning there can be no future meaning, for each projected future, each dream or vision, becomes a potential repeated past of nothingness. One runs the risk of creating the same kind of scorn presently pervading one's present and the past. The past does not contain the liberating seeds of present meaning and hopefulness, for those seeds were not sown. The past is seen rather as an omnipresent, nagging weight, holding down one's progress.

A good example of what I am talking about can be found in the experiences of battered children as adults, living with their own children. Often all that is known to correct or control their own children is battering, a repetition of their own childhood experiences. The battering is a way in which they relive their past by knocking their children into the future, which for some may be death. Only by living under supportive conditions in the present at some time can they experience the inanity and hopelessness of their past and create present and future conditions of support for themselves and their children.

Moreover, in relationships which foster human growth and unity within and without, we find the quality of vulnerability among those involved. Without vulnerability there can be no shared experience, for there is no receptivity to the other as reflecting a different unique reality. The paradox is that without being vulnerable to the uniqueness of the other, one's own uniqueness cannot be grasped. Life becomes much like steady contemplation in a mirror. Without experiencing interdependence, there can be no independence. The more we are linked, the more each can be his other different self, the freer each can become.

Punishment, in any form, destroys presence and any hope of human growth for it destroys vulnerability, the very possibility of interdependence. Punishment is a way of relating in the face of which the person being punished can never let up from holding on to the world as he or she has known it, can never prepare to relinquish the needs that once gave him or her insufficient definition (e.g., power) and become receptive to what exists presently. The punished is always forced to hide from the impact of the punishing agent, who also must live in a non-present, one-dimensional world for his or her own survival. One cannot punish and be present at the same time, for presence defies punishment. Each is forced, therefore, to become absent to each other.

The studies of relationship in prison and other social arrangements in which relationship is based on punishment demonstrate that wards and staff, supervisors and those supervised, helpers and their clientele, assume roles that enable them to abstract themselves from relationships of meaning and presence. Eugene Debs describes this process of self-abstraction in the prison:

The guard and the inmate cease to be human beings when they meet in prison. The one becomes a domineering petty official and the other a cowering convict. The rules enforce this relation and absolutely forbid any intimacy with the human touch in it between them. The guard looks down upon the convict he now has at his mercy, who has ceased to be a man and is known only by his number, while, little as the guard may suspect it, the prisoner looks down upon him as being even lower than an inmate. [19, 25].

The same distancing imposition of self upon another that Debs describes can be found in the family of today, the school, the medical center and the workplace in which relationship is treated as commodity. People organize in ways that inhibit intimacy, that create and maintain distance from each other as well as from their inner selves. The core of self that spells collective consciousness, connectedness with all that is human and creative is excised from one's sense of reality. Punishment supports its own unique form of separation from present reality. Punishment promotes the very schizo-existence that justifies its continuation. Contrary to the often-repeated proverb, revenge is never sweet.

In the defensive, abstract atmosphere that punishment creates, the possibility of self-awareness, of becoming more the self each is or wishes to be, whole and unified, is negated. There is no present meaning for both punished and punisher. Both giver and receiver suffer the same consequences, human humiliation and a separation from the human part of self. For both, relief from the destructive acts always lies somewhere in the future, outside the setting of the punishing atmosphere. One must escape to some other place, time, mind, to be free.

The act of punishing in effect fixes people into a past reality or projects them into an image of wholeness somewhere in the future, when debts will be paid in full and the debt collectors will be able to lay down their arms. Those who punish push to regain this lost Eden for society, by way of retribution, or to create the conditions for a new Eden, somewhere in the future, through deterrence; but little do they realize that any world based on debt is an illusion, and a fragile one at that. Such a future becomes for them, not a positive value or relationship, but a time, place, relationship based on the negation or cessation of the present, when their present nothingness and destruction will end. The process of punishing generates its own self over and over again. Present nothingness generates future nothingness. This has been the history of the American correctional system.

As far as any theory of correcting or justice goes, without shared experiences, without a present of meaning—when one's needs for survival, love, caring, being cared for, are being satisfied—there can be no meaningful resolution about one's future behavior and relationships. Only by living in the present can one begin to recognize one's feelings, values, goals, and needs as one's own and begin to negotiate in a responsible fashion a future of human concern for oneself. This way of life reflects a "more basic relation of time and community, namely, time as human arises from community. Men can recover a past only as they experience a community; men can work to create a future only from within a community. Men come to awareness before the face of other men and it is only because of this that they can delve into what nature gives them and what the possibilities are for a future" (Moran, 122).

19

PRESENCE AND HARM

A Matter of Time

The relationship between punishment and experience is confused by most people because of the rather awkward and limited concept of time we have inherited from mechanical models of time, developed from scientific fascination with the clock in the seventeenth and eighteenth centuries. For most people, the issue of time is not considered relevant to why we hurt each other. A view of relationship based on a mechanical perspective of time has helped most people to confuse living in the present with harmful behavior and therefore facilitated the rejection of the present as a valuable concept for understanding or living together harmoniously. A good example of the kind of confusion I am talking about can be found in a statement by Edward Banfield, who claims that the roots of crime and related urban ills can be found in a "present-mindedness" on the part of people, an orientation to life that is rooted solely in the present, resulting in an uncontrolled irresponsibility to self and others. He claims the slum dweller is "incapable of conceptualizing the future or of controlling his impulses and is therefore obliged to live from moment to moment. . .impulse governs his behavior. . .whatever he cannot consume immediately he considers valueless" (45–62). Contained in Banfield's statement and most statements that attempt to give behavior a time orientation is that they assume a mechanical model of time. This not only limits what can be said about the relation between person and time but supports class-based theories. It implies that those who engage in hurtful acts are so wrapped up in the present that they have no respect for the past or for the future. I would argue the opposite: that those who engage in hurtful behavior are people who do not live in the present but feverishly seek to escape from the present, to the past or future, there being for them no human experience or human hope in the present.

Banfield's statement about harmful behavior highlights a popular conception of time which is itself a major problem in our thinking about social life. For example, the belief about time that underlies such books as Toffler's *Future Shock* (1970) is that time is broken up into three parts—past, present, and future—and can be represented as a series of movable points on a straight line. "The present is imagined to be the one point which constantly moves forward while the past consists of points to the left of the present and the future is made up of points to the right of what is now present" (Moran, 119).

This linear conception of time generates such concepts as "time flowing" or "saving time" or "not enough time," as if time were a commodity, a dimension external to and controlling human experience. While ultimately this is true in relation to our mortality, I am assuming that death is not the dominant part of a person's present reality. Time is thought of as a matter of points accurately gauged by a mechanism in space (the pendulum) outside the subjective, human meaning, rather than as a way to express or represent experience. It is thought that people "save time" or "make progress" by eliminating some of the linear distance in life, by jumping over a certain number of line points. Time is seen as the controlling agent of human experience, something one has to counter-control for happiness or quality of life. One has to get to the future more quickly—that is, more quickly than others—for time in this context is competitive or comparative and therefore a form of aggression. One of the most ironic situations with respect to time as linear, as external to experience, can be found in the shouts of angry mobs in the squares of Great Britain in 1752 when the calendar was changed to the Gregorian: "Give us back our eleven days!"

The difficulty with this notion of time is that wholeness, happiness, quality of life are never present realities but always exist somewhere in the future or in someone else, which one must somehow catch up to as quickly as possible. This kind of thinking about time classifies forms of human misery such as crime, ignorance, and sickness as elements to be escaped from, for these bind a person to an unhappy present thereby negating progress to the all-important future.

Within this view of time happiness and progress have come to be viewed in relation to speed, to covering space on the time line. The faster one goes, the more space one covers, the more secure and happy a person supposedly is. As Chogyam Trungpa states: "Constantly we find ourselves slipping off the edge of a floor which had appeared to extend endlessly. Then we must attempt to save ourselves from death by immediately building an extension to the floor in order to make it appear endless again. We think we are safe on our seemingly solid floor, but then we slip off again and have to build another extension." (20). What most people fail to grasp about time, however, is that by shrinking time and space through speed, through the consumption of points, a person projects him or herself out of the present and thereby abstracts his essence of self from the safety of experience and the experience of safety. What a person desires as an end always eludes his or her grasp because of the means taken to that end.

Lewis Mumford provides from Buckminster Fuller a good example of the shrinkage of time and space and its effect on presence and human experience. Fuller talks about a sphere twenty feet in diameter, to represent transportation time-distance by, first, walking. When a horse is used, this sphere gets reduced in size to six feet; with the clipper ship it becomes a basketball; with the railroad it is reduced to the size of a baseball; with the jet plane, a marble, and with the rocket a pea and so on. If it were possible to travel at the speed of light, the earth would become a molecule, so that the traveler would be back at his starting point without the briefest sensation of having left it (1970:204) but exhausted nevertheless, exhausted to the point of self-destruction.

What is important about this illustration is the relationship between speed and experience as time. First of all, the greater the speed, characterized as movement away from present space, the less space and time there is for experiencing in the present, for one is always moving onward. The body in essence becomes a projectile for the consumption of points on the time line. Present experience, one's personal journey for meaning, is co-opted or sacrificed for some future possibility or reality, or some future set of events that appear to be preferable. Yet it is a set of events that never materializes, because once the next point is reached, it too must quickly be consumed and forsaken for another point or set of events farther down the line. A person's present or presence is always situated somewhere in the future, to the right of our imaginary linear time line. For a person to be successful he or she must always be other than he or she really is, moaning: "If only I could get rid of this thing, then I would be relieved, I would feel free."

Whatever reasons are offered as the official causes of crime and hurtful behavior (e.g., Banfield's present-mindedness), I find those involved in hurtful behavior to be besieged by a pressing emptiness with respect to the present. Toffler is wrong when he sees our societal problems as related to "future shock." In reality, the culture we now live in suffers from present shock. The hurting, harming person is someone who has nothing worth living for in the present, is not present to another, for there is no one worth being present to, worth living for, no community of concern. So we have only the constant struggle to escape from the enduring pain of this present reality through drugs, sound, consumption, power, the constant going elsewhere, like our hypothetical person speeding through the time line, even when it means consuming other people's lives, bodies, spirits. Ultimately it means our own consumption.

The hurting person—taken in both ways, hurting to others and personally suffering—is a person who turns away from the present. His is the kind of lifestyle LeGuin has characterized as that of a "variety seeker," a person who goes through life, from experience to experience, person to person, event to event, to fill the void, the lack of present meaning. This is Banfield's "present-minded" person for whom happiness means going through things, for whom human experience is equated with consumption, whether it be the consumption of others through power, or purchase. This going through things is itself a form of violence. Personal continuity is not found through mutual support or shared experiences but in the consumption of persons and things through privatizing them, making them private property. The world can never be a place to contemplate in the present, a place to share in the creation of, only a place to use things, to control, to eat up.

In short, to live in the present, to be present-minded, is to experience the presence of someone who cares, to experience self and life through relationships that have their grounding in present sharing even when it means struggle and pain. It is having one's human needs satisfied, or accepting the suffering that comes with the emptiness of loss. The person who is present experiences the mutuality and reciprocity of relationship, not only with those immediately present but also with those who have gone before as well as those who will come after. There is a connectedness with history. There is a strong sense of posterity. There is no rush to the future to capture one's lost past, for the future and the past reside within oneself. Time flows because one experiences.

20

HARM AS EXPERIENCE

A Matter of Power

I hope that it is evident from the discussion of time and experience that the hurting or harmful person is a person who must control or consume presence for survival, whose definition of quality of life is based on consuming others, the world around him or her. Life, self, others, are things to be traded for, bought, purchased, or transformed into the never-ending floor of Trungpa noted above, to allay the fear of falling off. For such a person, ownership becomes safety, the safest form of holding on to reality, for there is always a handy supply of consumable world and relationship to keep oneself in touch with reality. Monopolization becomes the ultimate security, the ultimate safety. Therefore power becomes the abiding principle in relationship, punishment its backup form for monopolization. The paradox is great, however, for through power and punishment, the means by which one hopes to bring about presence, one vacates or destroys the very presence one wishes to capture and appropriate, what will help to fill the insatiable holes of one's emptiness.

In the present discussion of harm and power, it is not my intention to develop a full-blown theory of criminality but to understand harm and power in relation to human experience, and then the tools or means that best facilitate human experience. One of the central problems in corrections is that most people who are concerned about these things have come to confuse idioms of control, the notion of being *in* control as opposed to being *out of* control. Therefore the state-certified tools for enhancing human experience (e.g., the school, the prison, medicine) are based on faulty assumptions and tend to harm both self and relationship. An example of how harm and power are interrelated will help to clarify what I am talking about.

The popular conception of the criminal rapist, to take one example, is that of a person who gets out of control and loses all sense of himself. He is Banfield's "present-minded" person. But this conception of the rape situation and harmful behavior generally is a false one. The rapist is a person not at all out of control but rather a person who cannot afford to lose any control, for a moment. The rapist must be totally in control of a given sexual experience, that is, monopolize sexual interaction with another. The rapist permits no negotiation of sexual relations on the part of the other or any shared experience, as is found between two sharing lovers. Only a fixed, power-based sexual arrangement, one that fits the rapist's conception of sexual relationship, is allowed.

The rape interaction then is a power-based relationship in which one person (the rapist) defines the boundaries, script, activities of the entire sexual drama from beginning to end, which only the rapist has the power to modify and renegotiate. The presence or sharing of the person being raped is not a requirement for the sexual interaction. And it should be noted that this power does not arise solely from the physical size of men or some innate male aggressiveness, as is often believed in our present society. We live in a society in which the male is conceived to be superior to the female (and I mean both biologically and conceptually), which generates a corollary conception that a man has a right to or monopoly over the female partner. The concomitant to this superior male identity is a conception of women as inferior, things to be used and discarded, carriers of children (male preferably) for family continuity, new resources for the power-based economy that thrives on this relationship of competition and distance.

In the same way we can look at the person who murders another as a person who must be totally in control of a life situation. The murderer sets himself up as the sole arbiter of who will live and who will not, through the use of power, by a monopoly over experience. Again, as in the case of the rapist, there is no negotiation permitted, no discussion of mutual needs or shared life, only the raw, and in this case total, destruction of another's presence. Harm, as I have argued throughout, boils down to a situation or an act when the presence of another is either denied or eliminated, as the other, representing an alternate and often painful reality to accept, is transformed into an object—temporarily or permanently. Those who use power at whatever level are farthest away from what is present, natural, and human.

The same is true for social institutions. The problem of harmful behavior is not simply the personal acts which law or the state say it is or is not, for that allows the state itself to remain beyond the definition of harm, beyond incrimination. Harm must be seen in the more comprehensive context of the use of power and punishment as a means to relate, whether by people or institutions. The violent, hurting acts of people and the violent, punishing, controlling acts of the state are of the same genre. In each instance the acts reflect an attempt to monopolize the boundaries of human interaction, to control relationship by controlling or consuming presence. Power is a way to rule another's fate as if it were a commodity for consumption. The state-defined criminal is a person judged to have transgressed the state-defined dosage of power. The state-defined criminal or harmful person is punished not for violating human presence with power, though this is what occurs, but for his or her use of monopolized power, which the state, through the instrumentation of law and custom, attempts to monopolize for itself. The state is not against men's control of women, for example, but against men's monopolization of this relationship. It is for this that the criminal is punished, for attempting to monopolize control and power in securing experience or property, in the way the state does.

Allow me to repeat myself. State-defined legal reality has the criminal defined, processed, and punished not for violating the personal freedom of another or for denying to someone his or her presence to share in experience, because the state, industry, and corporations which the state regulates thrive in this way. Rather, the criminal is punished (and the whole repertoire of dramas in the criminal justice system is set up for this purpose) for behaving in the way the state does. The criminal is punished for acting as a counter-state, an alter-state, for using total power to control the movement or presence of people or property in an absolute way, the way the state does. The criminal is a person who attempts to generate or allocate experience from without and to control presence rather than negotiate mutually the definition and satisfaction of human, present needs. The criminal, as in the case of the state, defines from the outside the boundaries of experience. This is essentially the kind of activity the state engages in and why the state must eradicate the criminal, for the state is a criminal whose turf is being violated by one of its own kind—the power users. In effect, the state views the criminal as a business competitor, as another fledgling power broker, an entrepreneur whom the state must squelch and put out of business, so as to insure its own monopoly over experience. In the same fashion, on a somewhat different level, the so-called deviant is punished or stigmatized by the state and its array of institutions for incarnating in his person an alternate reality, one that makes a mockery of the power game set up by the state. The state's activity is to interest that person, through force of law, in the state's power game to live by the state's power rules, rather than by rules self-defined. The state is against self-regulation of any sort. And anyone who refuses and who lives contrary to the state is invited to live in the house of the state, the prison-asylum complex.

Kennedy has summed up the relation between the acts of the criminal and the acts of the state: "If crime and punishment are injurious to life, then each belongs to the same class of conduct and should be viewed as two independent species of harm" (1). Both the state and the criminal are in the same business, the regulation and destruction of presence through the monopolization of determining and satisfying needs. Both forms of activity make community an impossibility, for both assert that using power is the only profitable and therefore human way to relate to satisfy needs.

It is, of course, possible to argue that the state's concern in punishing people is aroused because people violate the sanctity of life and therefore deserve punishment. This is the state's claim. But the state's concern is not with the violation of the sanctity of life or human presence, only with the sanctity of its own power and allegiances. There are many examples of state regulation and control that support this contention. For one, in family relationships the state's concern is not with fostering free agreement or equality among family members (e.g., between partners, between parents and their children) but in fostering and maintaining hierarchical, sexist, ageist roles, roles that deny or constrain sanctity of life. Family relationships are not supported that are based on the principle of to each according to his needs but according to the principle of to each according to his merits or works, according to his political-economic standing. State ideology does not support the notion that all persons in a family, regardless of age, sex, and income level, are equal and free to negotiate their own view of reality, to learn as they wish, to medicate themselves as they wish, but are equal to the extent that they produce in the market, to the extent that they live by state norms. Personal value is based on one's works or merit—that is, consumption power. Only those who produce in the progress or scarcity economy have the right to establish their own proper feelings, values, and goals. Those who do not produce are subject to a priori definitions of self and reality by those who do.

The women's movement in this century essentially was an attempt on the part of women, female partners, mothers, to escape from male-defined roles of reality and to claim equal access to definitions of reality. The error of many women who shared in the movement, however—as is becoming increasingly clear—was not grasping that getting power is not the solution to their oppression, for power as a means destroys the intimacy they desire most. The more fundamental need in human relations, in the family, between partners, was missed—namely, the need for the dissolution of power and for living by an economy of relationship based on the well being of each, not as a matter of right but as a matter of needs. One is human and equal not because the state says so but because one has needs. Needs make us equal.

State support for a power-based society is evident in other ways. For example, those who live according to state-directed power specifications are variously rewarded. For one, they are spared the stigmatization of representing an alternate reality—that is, insanity or treason. Also, the state provides economic inducements for conformity in the form of tax deductions. There are in fact penalties for those who do not live according to the specifications of the nuclear family. A family with a working wife-partner in which separate tax returns are filed is taxed more, as are those who are single and divorced. Being single, for example, can be construed as an abstention from or resistance to performing state-defined roles in the hierarchical family structure and may be punishable.

At the same time the father-husband who leaves the family is punished by being required by law to pay alimony and child support not for denying meaningful human experience to others but for breaching the sexist-power relations sanctioned by the state. He is not engaged in the up-keep of his property! If the state's concern were with maintaining solidarity within the family unit, regardless of sex or age, then we might expect women as a matter of course to be required to pay alimony also when they chose to leave the family. But this is not the case. Men who leave the family are viewed as also deserting the state and the performance of their economically profitable roles. They are, once again, punished for not carrying out their power roles of sexist control. Any alternate reality, any renegotiated reality and new relationships, are punishable by way of the male being forced to pay for his past.

We can find another example of the state's support of power-based society in the state-certified school. The young person who finds state-credentializing education debilitative and destructive, and who chooses to leave school to search for meaning elsewhere, is adjudicated truant by the state and judged to be in need of supervision, or punishment and help. Those young people who choose to leave the family are adjudicated promiscuous, incorrigible, delinquent, runaway, and judged to be in need of state supervision and punishment to deter them from these and similar acts. These deserters are punished because they too attempt to transcend the acceptable power relations sanctioned by the state.

To assert one's human need to live by one's own feelings, values, goals, and to claim the human right to negotiate one's conception of reality as one experiences it, are tantamount to challenging the definitions of use of power prescribed by the state. To seek experiences beyond state-prescribed drugs, beyond state-prescribed roles is criminal. A person is judged criminal or deviant because he refuses to experience as the state directs. It is no different from the situation of the rapist, the state punishing anyone who attempts to transcend in some way or compete in some way for state definitions of reality.

21

MEANS ARE ENDS

Toward the Dissolution of Power

When we examine the productive tools of our present society in relation to their ability to foster personal integration and social unity, we see that their foundations are rooted in power and competition, the exploitation of nature and persons for abstract ends such as progress, community safety, health, or justice that have no foundation in the day-to-day struggle and well-being of people. As Lewis Mumford notes: "In terms of the power system, progress means simply more power, more profit, more productivity, more paper property, more publicity—all convertible into quantitative units" (1970:167).

To use power as a principle for relationship—whether the relationship is between person and environment or between persons—is to share in the cultivation of the despair and violence one is attempting to dissolve. For correctionalists it is a sharing in the creation of the very social conditions that bring about the social harm they claim they are attempting to eliminate. Power is never a means to health or safety or unity. In fact, power as a tool only threatens "the physical structure of the universe, undermines our participation in useful activity, deadens our creative imagination, usurps our autonomy and threatens the diversity of human language, culture and beliefs" (Tifft, 1978:10). Sharing in the pursuit of an abstract goal such as "community safety" or a "crime-free society" is simply one more justification for continuing the present and personal exploitation of others.

To use power is to share in the domination of both nature and people, Jerome states, "as might a rapist, getting what passed for love the only way he knew how, knowing all the while he was destroying the possibility of real love, like a drowning man compulsively breathing water, unable to wait a panicky moment until he can breathe air" (173). To base one's life on power is to invade and violate the sanctity of others and to foreclose the possibility of unity within oneself and with others. Power militates against the natural impulse of people, which is to "grow, change, to rectify error as a stalk seeks sunlight, to seek self-actualization through symbiotic relationship with other self-actualizing and very diverse individuals (as healthy flowers require healthy bees, and vice versa). Mechanistic controls and constraints interrupt this process" (Jerome, 256).

The use of power is not simply a phenomenon of the state or bureaucratic organizations even though we may describe them as power-based. The use of power reflects a deeply personal choice on the part of individuals. It reflects the choice of individuals in the development of tools for relating to others by way of competition, greed, and exploitation. Social tools are no more than the collective ethical choices of people. In a very concrete way each of us who engages in bossing, inspecting, classifying, supervising, registering, ordering, specifying, policy making is involved in the use of power and shares to some degree or other in human depletion, in the denial of freedom and creativity to both self and others. Those who share in these kinds of activities in a very real way share in the production of harms of a civilization they speak of abstractly as something "out there." They share in creating the social conditions that deny to themselves and to others the possibility of spiritual rejuvenation.

Many people aware of their use of power and its effects argue that it is a necessary means to an end that is ultimately humane and freeing, a temporary means to free themselves from the oppression they presently experience through power-based, hierarchical relationships. Getting a share of power, they assert, will free them from the present use of power by others, enabling themselves to become all they wish to be. But one of the ironies of power is that there is never any "making it" so that a person can be free from its domination. In power relationships one must continue to exercise power to prove one's potency and alleged superiority. The continual creation and maintenance of domination facades becomes an essential ingredient of day-to-day living. One must continue to create and market power personas in the continuing drama of fear and paranoia, so that one will not be overtaken by another more powerful person.

If we have become a helpless society, addicted to therapies, pills, chemicals, prisons, bureaucracy, and the state, if these have become our tools for self-modulation, it is because people choose to live as lifelong combatants in these power and control games, wasted away by strident competition. The tension and anxiety that persist from childhood to old age are the result of the always immediate sensation, that one's opponent or one's self will get "out of control"—that is, have to use power to the point of destruction. There is the danger that one may become so out of touch with one's personal resources that one's only option will be to destroy the other.

Power relations breed this constant fear of being overwhelmed by another, so that a person must always be on guard lest he or she be victimized by the next person moving up the potency scale. Those who use power, therefore, live with the ever-pervasive fear of losing their identity or of being swallowed up in their pursuit of progress. They can never reveal their true feelings or beliefs or express with vulnerability their real needs. One's true feelings that reflect dependency and helplessness are viewed as potential sources of profit for another. Statements of need are not viewed as expressions of one's unique self and the material by which we bond ourselves together but as forms of weakness or sickness, the very aspects of a person power relations are supposed to curtail or eliminate. The history of power relations points to the opposite as true: power cripples, power reinforces dependency, power addicts a person either to wielding new forms of power or to submission to its blows.

Those who are objects of power and control may respond by way of protest for a while but soon burn out. Limiting themselves to private, individualized solutions, they begin to manufacture a series of submissive gestures that assert to their superiors that they are being controlled, are being enslaved successfully. It is the manufacture of these gestures of madness that Thomas Szasz describes, the manufacture of insanity gestures or escape valves for one's survival in what is deemed a survival-less living arrangement. Visions, acts, gestures, sentiments that suggest wholeness, freedom, and quality of life are covered deep beneath the indignity of submission-for-survival, a make-believe survival, for there is no such thing as survival without freedom.

The ultimate response of persons to power-based relations is inevitably detachment and withdrawal. Often these become the only available resources people see themselves as having for protecting their core self within the power conditions. The whole school of human relations management that emerged at the beginning of this century was acutely aware of this human retreat or withdrawal process and its effect on corporate production rates. Organizational theorists attempted to develop theories of participation which would help management to retrieve the energy lost through the detached presence of their workers. Through "human relations" management would help workers to get in touch with the dissenting parts of self, so that those workers might reintroduce those detached parts of self, employ their whole person toward increased productivity. Such theories, as far as I can tell, have never been developed with an understanding of the well being of those involved in the work, for their autonomy and creativity. The human relations school of management with its benevolence thinking serves as a valuable mask for the true concerns of management, the increased use of power over workers' lives. Managerial strategies show no sensitivity to the fact that people spend their entire lives trying to guess the mind of their bosses. Any talents individual workers might have are appreciated only as they fit into existing power conditions, for creative expression would mean having workers transcending the fixed, limited boundaries required of power relations, making a mockery of such a regulating, certifying existence. Therefore theories that support worker commitment to a life's work, to one's own life, remain unwritten. What is essentially human becomes the decaying core for growing insanity, exhibited in the clichéd existence of "I only work here!" or "I'm just here for a degree!" After a while many of these people begin to develop an institutional shuffle.

Those who continue to struggle for a period of time in this assumed role of absent self find that their planned protest or detachment soon begins to turn into a real self-effacement and self-deprecation. They begin to believe that they have no conviction, cannot act as persons directing their own lives, much less influence others and the world around them. The imposed assessment of who they are—processable raw materials—is soon fulfilled in fact, for they find themselves increasingly immobilized by the fear of failure, of trying things on their own. They are beset with the ever-pervasive despair of the continued nothingness of self. This person soon believes, as Rollo May states, that "since what he wants and what he feels can make no real difference, he gives up wanting and feeling" (28).

The result is that people steadily become empty abstractions, objects to be depleted by cunning production or systems analysis experts. They soon find themselves without feeling, without wanting, without dreams, without visions pointing to new lands to set sail to. They lose what is essential to the human struggle, their dreams, and the maps that chart for them their own vision of what a correct world is. There is no journey of life to be traveled, for the risk in moving is too great. The world, people, human relationships, are believed to be untrustworthy, unrewarding, non-supportive. They begin to mirror the faceless artillery of an economy they support through submission and indifference. In short, they become their own living dead, out of touch, devoid of intimate relationships, losing all feeling and presence. They take on the very conditions of our culture, becomes heirs to the pervasive carceral, imprisoned by schizo-existence.

And for those who spend their lives getting into power, there is soon the realization that quality of life with power, is no different from their previous life without power. The detestation of others that accompanies the power struggle upward, continues as they look downward. Only the locus, the vantage point of detestation, changes between the mutually hostile groups, those with and those without the power, as Tolstoy illustrates:

The one suffer from dependence on and hatred of those who rule over them, the others suffer from fear and feelings of contempt and ill will towards those over whom they rule, and others again from consciousness of the precariousness of their situation, from those endless utmost cruelties which are engendered and erupt from time to time, but without ever stopping the smoldering conflict between the two mutually detesting camps.

With power it is impossible to be or become a person of conviction, for one never has anything to believe in, much less anyone, only the maintenance of one's future status and one's ability to wield power in novel ways. One is always drained of energy by a fragile self-conception that is kept from full view of others. In male-female relations, for example, males must support the tensions that arise from their superiority complex by imprisoning females. They expand their shaky identities by defining, socializing, and forcing females into passivity and emotionality. Women find themselves obedient to men, with warped conceptions of self as woman or human being, through financial dependence and isolation. They live in anguish, loneliness, isolation, and despair. They "are taught the denial of self; women 'learn how to "lose" (themselves) in order to "win" (love and economic security)'; and then to discover they cannot exactly win anyway" (Chesler and Goodman, 3).

Consequently, with power one can never be free or truly independent, for the essential ingredients of interdependence and free agreement are missing. Power persons can never come to take a stand on life, because life is not a concern to them, only the depletion of people and natural resources, all seen as materials to be wasted for their own enhancement and profit. Their major concern is maintaining their position of control, which is always fragile and always changing according to the current needs of the power struggle, not those of people. Not taken into account is that this commitment to the domination and control of another is commitment to the domination and control of oneself, for there remains absent the possibility of oneself being the vulnerable locus of self-direction and self-regulation. Homage is always paid to a reality outside one's self.

While power as a force external to relationship is at the level of the most anti-human reality, we can also speak of the power that results from shared presence, the strength that comes from relationships based on cooperation, from shared realities, shared pain, shared healing, shared joys. I am not referring to power as a means here but rather to the power of experience, what results from the mutual aid we provide for each other. This entails the dissolution of power and competition as a means to any end.

We can gain some insight into mutual aid through an understanding of the pair of words active/passive, with which power and mutual aid are so integrally intertwined. Power as a means assumes a dichotomy between these words, a polarity between active and passive. The world is a configuration of distinct subjects and objects. A person is either active or passive, controller or controlled, dependent or independent, superior or inferior, producer or consumer, boss or subordinate. People, nature, relationship, are viewed as objectified raw materials to be processed, transformed, managed into some end product. The most common example of this polarity is contained in the belief that men are active and women are passive, or, in James Q. Wilson's terminology, that people are either "wicked" or "innocent." While those for whom the use of power is a source of profit would argue that people are one or the other, either biologically or naturally, I would argue that this polarity arises from the very use of power, from the principles of an economy in which the polarity of sexuality or goodness is a source of profit.

Active and passive are related pairs of words (we spoke of innocent/wicked, sane/insane, criminal/law-abiding), are not in reality polar but are mutually arising qualities within a person, within a relationship, or for that matter within the universe. They are relational, and to the extent that they are understood this way, it is possible to understand the interdependent quality of life, thereby opening up the way to the dissolution of power and to the use of mutual aid as an alternative for healing social divisions. Understood relationally, the concepts of active and passive necessarily imply each other, as giving implies receiving, as space implies bodies, as there can be no environment without organisms. No person is ever really totally active or totally passive in relationships that are personally fulfilling. People are both active and passive simultaneously, the intensity of each dimension differing according to ever-changing needs and circumstances. Any human experience requires an integration of the active and the passive in us, so that there is a give-and-take quality at any given moment. Human activity requires a simultaneous passivity or receptivity to what is happening as one acts, else the other, whether it be a person or nature, turns into an object, an opponent, a source of self-satisfaction, raw material to be exploited.

In human relationships that are warm, caring and mutually supportive the active and passive engage each other and transform each other in a transactional sort of way. Neither aspect of self is hierarchically valued as better or more essential, for each has positive value only when the other is present and given opportunity for expression. As Moran states:

The active in one person meets the passive in another, but the coming forth of the passive is a kind of activity. The weakness of one calls forth the strength of another which makes the original weakness a sign of strength (that is, what calls forth strength is stronger than strength). In turn, the original strength is revealed as weakness (that is, what has to be called forth by weakness is weaker than weakness). [110]

This point seems to have been missed by many who have shared in the women's movement. In their protest against the superior conception of men in our present economy, women generally have sought to imitate the active-aggressive qualities of men (e.g., by getting the same jobs as men, for the same pay as men). What many have overlooked, however, is the long-hidden activity that exists in their passive qualities, a kind of activeness that alone can draw from men the passive parts of themselves, which they have forfeited to become bosses in a machine-based, inhuman economy. Rather than each sex attempting to compete with the economically profitable qualities that exist in the other, each might begin to understand the power that exists in the active/passive balance in themselves, as well as the power that can exist in the active/passive balance between men and women.

To prefer or hierarchically order active over passive or vice versa in some fixed, a priori, absolute way is to destroy the possibility of its opposite emerging, for the ever-changing presence of the one brings forth the intensity and quality of the other. Both are rhythmically and organically related when mutuality exists. The paradox is that the greatest strength in relationship comes forth when persons meet at the point of their weakness, for the revelation and presence of weakness calls forth strength from the other—unless weakness is profitable, as it is in our present culture. In our present culture we do not come forth at the point of weakness, at the point where we must engage face-to-face those who have hurt or need others. Rather, we shove them off to prisons or asylums or homes or centers to hide them away. If we are not a strong culture, it is precisely for this reason, that we do not face our weakness head-on. We rely on professionals who novocaine our fears and charge us money for what disables us. Only when the weakness I am talking about finds the necessary support to be understood and accepted as part of life, can healing begin, is unity possible. Otherwise, unification of self and social unity remain an illusion.

Rarely is this kind of shared presence, at the point of weakness, evident, except under conditions of mutual aid, for it requires admissions of self that are non-admissible in a competitive, self-interest economy. When self and relationship are viewed in the context of profitable services, weakness and dependency like crime, insanity, sickness—must be denied, hidden, certainly not openly owned up to or shared with others. This is where the prison, the asylum, the hospital comes in. To admit failures within a capitalist society is regarded as a liability to one's future economic or political strength, to one's advancement in the market, on the time-line, elsewhere. We settle for managed detachment and withdrawal.

It is foolish to expect support for the expression of mutual aid within existing institutions, for the principles inherent in mutual aid threaten the management and maintenance of people ideology which power institutions are structured for. Nor is it possible simply to remain silent in the face of existing power as a way out, for silence and detachment are forms of assent to what is happening. Regardless, the suppression of one person ultimately means the suppression of us all, for one's own attempts at establishing some sort of quality of life are thwarted always. At any rate, managers will seek those who live by detachment and will sooner or later demand acts of submission for continued employment. It happens every day in the workplace and the school, in every situation where hierarchy exists. It is increasingly the case within the new realism, triage economy, where gestures of submission to officialdom are required for continued employment.

It is of little avail to suggest reform in professional organizations (e.g., watchdog agencies) or capitalist social structure (e.g., planned capitalism) or to modify structures through more advanced or progressive managerial strategies; for reform itself is part of power. Organizational reforms feed upon themselves, continually inviting more of the endless perfection exercises that the failing system invites and thrives upon. Each of us, if we wish to be free, if we wish to have human experiences and create communities of concern must, as Mumford notes, recognize that "the changes that will restore autonomy and initiative to the human person lie within the province of each individual soul." (433). It will be in the social context of our own search for freedom and community that the foundation stones for a safe society will be set down. If we have concerns for social justice, we must begin to extricate ourselves from the power complex, from all relationships based on power, from the use of power in our lives. "Each of us, as long as life stirs in him, may play a part in extricating himself from the power system by asserting his primacy as a person in quiet acts of mental and physical withdrawal—in gestures of non-conformity, in abstentions, restrictions, inhibitions, which will liberate" us from supporting structures that create schizo-existence (Mumford, 1970:433). It is not a move toward other forms of power or other forms of government but toward tools that reflect self-determination and self-regulation. It is a move toward spiritual rejuvenation.

I am talking about a way of life more than a lifestyle taken on—capitalism has survived this long on its production of lifestyles—a way of life which rests on a sense of the holy, the mysterium of life. This is the opposite of owning and possessing.

One is no longer obsessed by the principles of having objects, self, nature, or another person. In no longer packaging, marketing, selling and consuming self or others, one is no longer obsessed with being or becoming free from everything and everyone. Rather, one is free to exercise naked relationships, to be, in a world without the irons of domination-subordination, and the feelings of superiority-inferiority. [Tifft, 1978:13]

One is free to experience continuous spiritual rejuvenation, sharing experiences and experiencing sharing.

These experiences and feelings of solidarity are not fostered in structural conditions in which people are means but in conditions where they

are ends, sacred and equal; wherein stratification and hierarchy if present are situational and temporary; wherein the division of labor is symbiotic and yet self-directed independent; wherein there is personal and interpersonal stability and yet constant change, as each person continuously crashes through new barriers while building new foundations; wherein persons are recognized as unique, different and at once humanly similar. [Tifft, 1978:13]

Kropotkin describes the foundations for a conception of life radically different from those based on power: "The higher conception of 'no revenge for wrongs,' and of freely giving more than one expects to receive from his neighbor, is proclaimed as being the real principle of morality—a principle superior to mere equivalence, equity, or justice, and more conducive to happiness" (1902:299).

I V

MUTUAL AID

The Restoration of Connectedness through Needs, Literacy, Hands, Free Agreement

There was the time when we was on the lan'.
There was a boundary to us then.
Ol' folks died off, an' little fellas come,
An' we was always one thing-
We was the fambly-kinda whole and clear.
An' now we ain't clear no more.
I can't get straight.
They ain't nothin' keeps us clear. . .
We're crackin' up, Tom.
There ain't no fambly now.

John Steinbeck

22

MUTUAL AID ECONOMICS

Needs-based economy

The history of relieving human misery, whether we call it social harm, personal hurts, poverty, insanity, unemployment, in either individualized or collective ways, demonstrates rather forcefully that correcting means revolution and rejuvenation and as such is intertwined with economics, scarcity, and human needs. After a historical analysis of corrections as punishment, Rusche and Kirchheimer came to the simple but profound conclusion that "every system of production tends to discover punishments which correspond to its productive relationships" (5). That is, the tools designed for safety, for correcting relationship, get their definition from the tools we create for producing. To state it in another way, we can say that our relationship to the earth, through the work of our body and intellect, sets our definition of health and sickness as well as the tools for restoring that health when it breaks down in some way (e.g., crime, insanity, starvation).

As I mentioned at the beginning of this book, to begin a discussion of corrections within the framework of economics, human needs, and work seems to most people, particularly professional correctionalists, to be a grand leap off the subject, away from what is "practical." This is a striking irony in the work of correctionalists today. They propose theories for correcting relationship through systems, scientific method, the abolition of class conflict, or more equal and certain application of punishment (e.g., just deserts and fixed sentences), while rejecting human needs, the needs of the universe in which we produce to meet these needs. They wind up, therefore, producing theoretical abstractions. All the major theories of the twentieth century that have attended to crime and punishment issues have had their foundation in abstractions, the abstractions of political organization or state bureaucracy, not the everyday recurring needs of people.

What we see historically then is social theory laid upon social theory, in which the assumption persists that "the problem of social order may be solved, practically and intellectually, without clarifying and focusing on the problem of scarcity, with which economics is so centrally concerned." (Gouldner, 94). This lack of "clarifying and focusing" on economics, particularly on the part of professionals, can no longer be tolerated under the claim that economics makes no difference to how we relate to each other, when in fact this relationship between economics and interpersonal relations is understood perfectly well in the private lives of people. One simply needs to think of the rising cost of staying alive, the work needed to be done, and how these factors of cost and work influence family or interpersonal relations. To exclude economics as a factor (not *the* factor) in attempting to understand or adjust human relationships is to support a perpetually intoxicated way of life, a drugged existence. Perhaps, as with any addiction, it is courage we need to introduce some sense of political economy into our thinking about social life, and in particular, work.

For any individual to persist in excluding economics is to live an illusion that fosters personal and social imprisonment. It is in fact a withdrawal from any serious attempt to bring about personal growth, social unity and the sane society which people who make a living from such ideas claim is their objective. The humanity of a person, of his or her work, can be measured by its concern with a social ideal, in which theories about personal and social unity are linked to everyday matters in their own lives—the present. All who propose solutions for our living together cooperatively "must have one foot in the present world of routine survival mechanisms, fears, prejudices, misconceptions, and brutality practiced at all levels of society" (Mankoff, 300-301).

Let me restate. To develop theories of correcting relationship on any level, whether it be toward producing safety or fostering social unity, an individual must begin to state to him or herself some basic facts about human relationship. First, that how we set about to work for food, how we set about to create physical and emotional warmth for ourselves, determines the nature of the boundaries we set for both health and disability in our society, whether we call that disability misery, hunger, crime, madness, sickness, or dependency. Each of us, by the way of life we choose to lead, shares in the design and use of the tools to be used in meeting our collective needs—both producing and correcting tools. Each of us then creates the state, the prison, when we refuse to face self-sufficiency in our own lives when we refuse to recognize that the struggle to be human and safe is a cooperative struggle. If we work for food and warmth by means of power-based relationships, through stranger-enhancing relationships, we create the social institutions that foster relational distances between sexes, age groups, races, and classes. We share in the creation of greed, exploitation, and violence which we then create the state to stamp out.

The ideology of state-directed corrections, criminology, and political science has supported capitalist, competitive social arrangements by denying this relationship between economics, harm and correction. Historically, the state has maintained through the instrument of law that crime, madness, and human misery are not economic, social-structural issues but solely issues of personal and group pathology. Similarly, state ideology maintains that severed relationship (e.g., between rich and poor, between humans and their environment) can be restored by systems of professionally managed activities, services, and goods. The relationship between the means of production and the tools of safety is masked even more when we accept professionally managed warmth over that which comes with the suffering of a personal but shared responsibility for each other. This explains why most efforts in the area of corrections have been a search for idols. Theories, practice, ideals, have never had a human, face-to-face basis for action.

In redesigning our present tools so as to restore community health, it is not sufficient to state that some people steal, some murder, some rape, some are lonely and frightened to the point of immobilization, and to go about helping or treating them, when every politically sanctioned relationship, every tool of production and correction we can think of in this capitalist economy based on power fosters exploitation, depletion, and waste. The reality we must grasp is that we live in a culture of severed relationships, where every available institution provides a form of banishment but no place or means for people to become connected, to be responsible to and for each other. It is a foolish expenditure of human energy to continue to design and maintain tools to correct personal divisions in the human community when the economic system in which these divisions occur depends for its economic survival upon the continuing production of these divisions in the form of guilts, neuroses, psychoses, violence, waste, for its economic survival. This is the harsh reality we must face. To correct violence, crime, madness, and their everyday satellite manifestations is first to correct the pervasive divisions and disablement in our own lives.

Only by a personal commitment to radical restoration can we begin to recapture basic human competencies for healing the severed relationships that exist societally. What we must come to grips with is that we know very little about restoring severed relationships that emerge in the forms of crime and madness, because we know surprisingly little about the human.

We know very little about living with each other cooperatively, about human ecology and partnering for quality of life. Nevertheless, many correctionalists with deeply human concerns about creating community waste their time with tools that foster and aggravate severing. They work without understanding the political economic assumptions on which their tools are based, which more often than not specify that repartnering must not be done, that severed relationships must be maintained for the sake of the tools' survival.

We must begin to think about developing tools that are designed to restore partnerships with nature, with the soil, with each other. I am not advocating designing tools that will bring about the redistribution of wealth or the reallocation of resources. Uniform amounts of wealth can be distributed in a prison, and extrinsic resources can be uniformly allocated through the apparatus of the state and professional planners. The programs of the state in state-capitalist and socialist societies verify this. Imposed redistribution without participatory equality results in a more unified, politically perfected state—totalitarianism—not in more unified, humanly livable communities.

Concepts of justice and the tools for correction that are based on such principles as redistribution, equal rights, merits, or reallocation are still forms of justice as commodity, part of the productive network of a centralized system of control. Basic human competency to bring about unity remains in the hands of the owner, the holder, or the distributor of the tools or resources. And though increasingly we see distribution equalized through political equality and equality before the law (e.g., equal rights codes), both historical and cross-cultural evidence indicates that with the increase of law there is an increase in crime, appropriation, stratification, hierarchy, differentiation, and relational distance. (Tifft, 1979). Those who struggle for equality before the law or equality before professional forums, by their very arguments search for equality in mechanisms or tools that require schism and inequality for their survival. This should not be a surprising revelation, for rents, splits, and divisions emerge and persist in our own lives whenever and as long as someone or something remains in charge of our experiences. Human action toward solidarity that is indirect and dependent upon abstractions such as law, expertise, punishment, will only serve to reinforce the divisions they are designed to correct.

Indirect action of any kind brings us no closer to social intimacy and feelings of solidarity for each other. (Fischer, 1978:217). Our present society's addiction to state and professional expertise reveals this quite clearly. Indirect means always leads us away from unity, both personal and social, for the actions we engage in are never important for themselves but for some abstract goal such as social good or social progress. The tools we need to design are those that protect three basic values: survival, justice, and self-defined activity. These are tools based on direct action by way of mutual aid, based on the economic principle "to each according to his needs." Only through meeting each other's needs directly, which for our present phase of evolution means by a subsistence economy, will there be any movement toward personal connectedness, toward connectedness throughout the world. Only through direct, subsistence living are the structural conditions fostered whereby people are equal (through their needs), where stratification and hierarchy may be present but only situationally and temporarily. But "so politicized is our thinking, so focused to the motions of governmental institutions, that the effects of direct action to modify one's envirionment are unexplored" (Wieck). Mutual aid is considered to be a piece of political-social fiction.

The purpose of this book has been to reintroduce the tradition of mutual aid and its social principles which we have lost sight of, even though many have continued to practice mutual aid in their everyday lives. Mutual aid economics has at its foundation the belief that nature is essentially good, as is humankind—a part of nature. Similarly, it is based on the belief that there is an eternal interdependence among things, between one species and another, between the human and the non-human, and that the exploitation of one species, the denial or appropriation of species interdependence in any way has destructive ramifications for all. It is the belief that Judson Jerome expresses: "The welfare of one species depends upon the welfare of all others in the environment, even that of its natural enemies" (235). Without such a notion of interdependence as one's starting point, there is no hope for unity, for no aspect of life is ever regarded as valid in its own right and no human need is ever regarded as the authentic expression of being. There is never trust in the expression or resources of what is regarded as "other," whether the other be a person or a natural process. Another essential part of mutual aid economics is the belief that nature is sufficiently abundant to supply our needs when allowed to resonate in its own patterned anarchy, according to its own unique and diverse needs system. This holds true whether one is talking about the needs of people, of a river, a whale, a cloud, fields, mountains, or streams. Our present culture is one of violence because all aspects of nature including people are denied the full expression of their being, their needs, the material from which they discover their uniqueness. Each is barred from his fullness, his abundance of energy as means toward successful evolution.

Needs and well being are intertwined at every level of existence, both human and non-human. To begin to correct social problems without taking a larger view of cosmic reality is to begin one's work by dividing, tearing, splitting, and fracturing the foundations of one's efforts. "The earth and every tiniest thing upon it inevitably 'goes with' the sun, moon, stars. It needs them just as much as it needs, and consists of, its own elements" (Watts, 43). And because of the mutual interdependence of all things, each "will harmonize if left alone and not forced into conformity with some arbitrary, artificial, and abstract notion of order, and this harmony will emerge. . .of itself, without external compulsion" (44). This applies to relationship at all levels of existence, plant, animal and human. Any thinking about economics must take this into account from the outset.

As we press each other into service for marketable staples through the power relations of capitalism, we force each other out of our natural relational interdependence, creating a continuing distrust of each other. We have expected and continue to expect each other to act in accord with systems and managerial styles, processes, and systems of control that are designed not to meet human needs cooperatively but to ruin and co-opt other, less fit systems. The Hobbesian fear that within each person's unconscious there is an "inexorable principle," stems from defining people in terms of the needs of church, state, and industrial systems (Newman). And it is precisely this kind of treasonous exchange, human spontaneity sacrificed for church, state, or industrial ethics and their production quotas, that has kept us from safe communities, from evolving as communties of human concern.

Those such as Quinney (1978) who argue with fervor that the only moral praxis people can engage in today is to work toward a socialist state are mistaken. Instead of moving toward restoring primacy to human experience, to cooperative living, this kind of proposal moves toward a more refined, solidified state, which becomes in effect an omnipresent, omniscient correctional megaprison, a societal panopticon or carceral, as Foucault refers to it. Freedom is negated as all aspects of life become subject to state control, regulation, and certification, as communities, neighborhoods, and individuals become decentralized wards of the centralized state. Interdependence and freedom are sacrificed for new forms of hierarchy.

This continuing movement toward a carceral state is not a bit of political fiction I am drumming up to warn people about imagined hazards in some possible future society. It exists in the current expression of hybridized forms of socialist ideology, which are being developed to bail out capitalism's present manic-depressive behavior. I am talking specifically about planned capitalism. This form of socialism is the prescriptive social-economic psychiatrist, hired, as it were, to treat the reckless behavior of a suffering capitalist economy. Heilbroner, for one, argues in a cunning manner for state centrality at all costs, even human freedom, a good example of the inversion of life I have been talking about.

The processes of scientific development and technical application must likewise fall more and more under the guidance and, where necessary, the veto power of government. All this may require allocations of materials, prohibitions against certain kinds of investment or consumption activities, international arrangements, and a general sticking of the public nose into private life wherever that life, left to itself, threatens the very survival of the system. (1978a:71–72)

This kind of thinking is reflective of consummate robopathic existence. Is not the aim of work, of production, the satisfaction of the needs of all? for the well being of each of us? Is not our collective effort to meet the needs of each other for the purpose of enabling each other to be more free? to create? or more simply to be? Have we totally lost sight of the meaning of our coming and being together in the world?

If each of us desires to have a life in which all his or her forces, physical, intellectual, and emotional, may find full exercise, we must once and for all abandon the idea that such a life is possible or attainable on the path of disregard for the recurring needs of others. We must grasp the fact that no political-commercial organization, whether within a capitalist or socialist society, is sufficiently organic to provide for the needs of all. Its hierarchical demands cannot allow for the complexity of the universe as it is, for the diversity of people, for the interdependence of life, for they exist to reduce complexity and variety (Ward, 44–52). This reduction is perpetrated by way of all kinds of justifications—for example, the requirements of the socialist state, the needs of planned capitalism, etc.

Hierarchical, power-based organizations must rule out whatever spells diversity—namely, human needs. They must rule out the mystical or feeling or intuitive components of self as valid or real, those aspects of self that enable us to create or transcend and that insure possibility, for these spontaneous aspects of being minimize the absolute, one-dimensional nature of political organization. The human, mystical parts of self are viewed as competing with the needs of the political complex to control and regulate what is "other," and their presence therefore serves as the very justification for their being controlled, eliminated, or taunted by a "general sticking of the public nose into private life." Competition, justification, and centralized intervention go together. It is not surprising that alternative forms of organization have been overlooked, such as face-to-face federations, for amid the grandeur of hierarchy, as Proudhon noted over a century ago, they are "by nature peaceful and mild and play a self-effacing role in the political scene" (Proudhon, 1970).

The notion of need I have been talking about is not "need" as is ordinarily understood in today's commodity-based, expertise culture, where "the good citizen is one who imputes needs to himself with such convictions that he drowns out any desire for alternatives much less for the renunciation of needs" (Illich, 1978:31). Today needs are such that being unable rationally to pinpoint one's needs or not to have a sense of an individualized set of needs or to have to renounce one's needs is tantamount to losing one's identity. It is to lose one's means for relating hierarchically or consumptively. Need, to those who live by a consumer-commodity ethic, is an individualized offprint of a professionally concocted pattern of the model self, and to be ignorant or unconvinced of one's own needs has become the unforgivable anti-social act (Illich, 1978:31).

What is a need in this consumptive context is some thing, something established in an a priori fashion outside one's being or self (e.g., children have a need to be educated in a classroom). Similarly, satisfying this need (e.g., "I must get a degree from this institution of certification") is thought to be superior to being uncertain about one's needs (e.g., "Who am I?" "Does what I'm doing have meaning for me?"). To renounce one's needs or seek alternatives is treason (e.g., "What I need as a person is to know and understand what it means to be human, not credentials!"). Life's relationships are always prescribed. The relationship between one's consumer self and one's professional supplier, whether the supplier be a doctor, a teacher, or any servicer who works from the top down, is the essence or model of human experience.

Rather, our conception of what constitutes a need is not fixed, not a thing, but an expression of one's confusion, one's lack of self or the resources to be the self which one truly is or wishes to be. Need, therefore

is always expanding, and consequently we must expect that there will never be sufficient resources to completely satisfy each person's needs. In this circumstance, justice (or to each according to his/her needs) means an equal proportion of each person's needs should be satisfied. Each person should achieve the same well-being as every other. However, because people have varied needs and wants, resources should *not* be allocated in equal quantities to each, but rather in different proportions to different persons, according to their individual different needs. [Tifft, 1978:11]

This is not inegalitarian, for the principle of equality does not mean equal treatment, but rather that each person achieve the same level of well being as every other. And because each person has different needs and preferences, basic needs such as food and medicine and shelter should not be assigned in equal quantities, but rather in response to need. To give an example, suppose that musical instruments are being alloted and I prefer a piano to your guitar. If I receive a piano (even though it might cost three times more than your guitar), it is equal treatment—not in the sense of cost or dollars put out, but in the sense that the well being of each of us has been achieved.

Need is essential as the basis for a human economics, for it is that dimension of self or being that gives a person his or her uniqueness or difference—bodily, emotionally, and intellectually. It is through our needs, their recognition, expression, and satisfaction or denial, that we come to create, to be who we are. Through need or dependence we become free. It is also through shared responsibility for meeting needs and achieving the well being of each that we create solidarity, foster the social bonding that we call community. We feel safe among differences!

What is more, these dimensions of being we refer to as need are not solely human traits but exist throughout the natural world, in animals, plants, streams. Each part of the universe has its own unique needs and must be allowed to resonate in the form of these unique needs if each is to be fruitful and fulfilling. Without these unique forms of expressed self being present to all else—that is, to what is "other"—the interdependence and mutuality required for unity, harmony, and safety are voided. There is well being for no one.

Finally, we must recognize that it is through our needs that we are most fully a part of the human race. Need "qualifies" us, not status, wealth, or certification ribbons. We must remember that those who have hurt others are people in dire need, a situation that renders them the most human among us. It is they who remind us of who we are as a people, as a community, and it is them we must be especially attentive to with our presence.

Living according to the principle "to each according to his or her needs" requires settings, both work and living settings, where this presence is fostered, where caring relationships predominate, where feelings of commiseration, equality, and solidarity are engendered. Only by interacting with others and with nature as equals in need can there be life and justice. Only then is the essence and meaning of life disclosed, for each person exists in his or her fullness, in his or her most convivial or hospitable proportions. The bounty and power and resources of each is available to each other in interdependence. And this interdependence exists only when each is owned by no other. Privatization, ownership, control, are theft of interdependence and therefore of uniqueness, of existence.

Any kind of treatment or corrections or rehabilitation must be the restoration of severed connections, the renewal of the interdependence and partnerships that encourage personal worth and personal responsibility for life. Only by closing these severings that put us against each other can we begin to understand the harms we render against each other and begin to heal them. This requires our reimmersion in the natural world with the being of our primitive self. We must get close to the world of nature we have hidden ourselves from.

23

MUTUAL AID EDUCATION

Reading Nature As Literacy

When we look at the relationship humankind has had with nature historically, we see that until our present industrialized world human culture as a whole developed in an organic environment. Although in a "confused," mysterious, and often "unfocused" way, from the vantage point of scientific method and political organization, "the criteria of life prevailed everywhere and man's own existence prospered or failed in so far as a balance favorable to life was preserved among all organisms." Humankind lived in active partnership with plants and animals, imbued with a keen understanding or instinct that the simplest organisms had things to teach us about life. (Mumford, 1970:380) They were in fact a spiritual as well as practical guide to cooperative existence. As Eiseley notes: "Nature was actually as well read as an alphabet, it was the real 'tool' by which man survived with a paucity of practical equipment." (1970:59)

Kropotkin found the same to be true during his distinguished career as a naturalist and geographer. "The deeper we go into the study of primitive man," he asserted, "the more we realize that it was from the life of animals with whom he stood in close contact that he learned the first lessons of valorous defense of fellow-creatures, self-sacrifice for the welfare of the group, unlimited parental love, and the advantages of sociability in general" (1934:21). Primitive man learned an intimate sense of sociability and play from animals as well as the advantages of common work, a settled life, and permanent dwelling. The natural world of plant and animal was immanent, present in everyday existence. Primitive man "repeated these exploits of animals in his tales, embellishing the acts of courage and self-sacrifice with his primitive poetry, and mimicking them in his religious rites." (1934)

If we are to talk about human need or necessity, the true and unvarying necessity for our ancestors was immersion in nature, observing and grasping its organic movements and connectedness, not as a detached observer with an objective feeling about it all, but through a profound personal involvement as one of its struggling components, continually adjusting his or her cooperative efforts for survival and quality of life with others. Enforced literacy in the certifying classroom will never be able to produce this experience. It will only enslave us further by making assumptions about industrialized literacy that have limited historical bases, those in the written-read word tradition, the recorded word of imperial entrepreneurs and merchants (Kozol).

Through an awesome involvement in nature, the primitive person had value, present value, not because he or she produced or read in accord with the quotas of externally imposed systems, but because they were present as beings among other beings. Each person's being was an integral part of the whole because each provided presence to the whole. Each person had a sense of the necessity of his or her own presence for social unity and continued connectedness. Each person provided as well as received meaning. Where this partnership through presence was negated in some animal group or human community, the group began to fail in its struggle for life. Cooperative efforts disappeared. Finally the group moved toward social decay. And if the group did not return to the necessary partnership or interdependence, then it died out altogether (Kropotkin, 1934:31).

With the emergence of competitive-based, industrialized economies such as capitalism, a different consciousness has been rewarded. Social consciousness is fostered and rewarded that regards each person, each part of nature, as an independent self-subsistent unit. Social good, societal happiness, or social evolution is said to be advanced by giving free play to private ambition. Social relations are engendered in which each should receive the exact equivalent in value of what he or she brings to exchange. One's value or worth is measured by one's differential productive powers or cunning salesmanship, not one's being or presence. The result of this kind of thinking has been the severing of humankind's partnership with nature and the severing of each of us from one another. Increasingly our relationship has become one of hostile strangers. As people are forced to become literate in state-certifying schools, they become increasingly illiterate in reading nature, what it says about interdependence, needs, and living cooperatively. Rather than trust their own inclinations, needs, and experiences, they live by the literacy data produced by social scientists, themselves illiterate in the natural.

In the meantime land, water, sky, the earth, all the elements that once symbolized cooperation and mutual aid, have become raw materials only for economic proceeds—corporate, military, and scientific. Tools for survival, developed from this kind of world view are privatized and professionalized; the means for basic human cooperation and mutual aid are turned into commodities, services for sale. Literacy has been changed from a kind of relationship to an item, a commodity, something to be delivered rather than lived through by personal involvement in the universe, with others. We are witnessing what I refer to as the inversion of life, whereby the basic concepts of life are spoken about in the language of death and vice versa, where death is treated as life (e.g., funerals as a living commodity) and life is treated as death (e.g., triage economics as a living commodity).

Life continues to evolve as a war with nature—that is, as death. As we humans have become less able to speak to nature and less able to hear nature speaking to us, we have become less able to speak clearly to each other through our needs. What was once natural habitat and grounding for human speech, a source of unity even in the worst of times, is valued now in terms of political control and economic salability. It has resulted in a war of each against all, lighter skinned against darker, younger against old, men against women, parents against children,—all the divisions that have been addressed throughout this book. Similarly, as partnership with nature becomes even more privatized in the form of nation-state property (e.g., oil rights), human relationships become a matter of national property, creating greater divisions between mind and soul in the form of neuroses, psychoses, and megatechnic fears.

As social-political divisions become greater, the farther removed from human consciousness is our partnership with nature as a necessary condition for survival and social evolution. This consciousness is hardly existent throughout the world today. Denying that the severing of our partnership with nature has consequences for our everyday lives and construction of social reality, we pursue the insane, the criminal, the deviant, as nervous pirates might pursue a lost treasure. State officials are able to continue to define harm solely in terms of personal pathology, as if frail humans hurting each other interpersonally were the cause of severed relationships in the cosmos, as if correcting these personal hurts could possibly restore the severed cosmic partnerships and bring about social unity among nations. The flaw of humankind is believed to reside solely in persons, not in the way we have structured our economic relationship with nature or our political relationship with each other internationally. While the resolution of interpersonal conflicts and hurts is a critical and recurring problem of social life, efforts in this regard mean little if they are not shared by all and viewed in a context of shared responsibility for life. It is foolish and simplistic to keep punishing exiles for behaving like exiles toward each other when in fact there is no homeland for them in which to be welcomed.

Though social progress is heralded as the goal of capitalist and socialist economies, the result has been the opposite as far as human evolution is concerned. Individual freedom has

remained both in theory and practice, more illusory than real. As to the other domains—political, intellectual, artistic—it may be said that in proportion as economic individualism was asserted with more emphasis, the subjection of the individual—to the war machinery of the state, the system of education, the mental discipline required for the support of existing institutions, and so on—was steadily growing. [Kropotkin, 1934:27]

In fact, the progressive utopia that capitalist economies have to show is a utopia of anxiety, pills, isolation, and fears of annihilation, a necessary and sufficient condition for a totalitarian state. "Totalitarianism appeals to the very dangerous emotional needs of people who live in complete isolation and fear of one another" (Arendt, 1978:18). Though loaded with all the mechanical-commodity accessories and professional services that come with progress, the modern person moves about in a world in which he has lost all the instinctual ability that comes with the expression of needs. Supported with all the machinery that will fly them into galactic utopias, people sit immobile from the ever-present fears of self and cosmic extinction. Each

earns money, typically, as a specialist, working an eight-hour day at a job for the quality of consequences of which somebody else—or perhaps more typically, nobody else will be responsible. And not surprisingly, since he can do little else for himself, he is unable to entertain himself, for there exists an enormous industry of exorbitantly expensive specialists whose purpose is to entertain him. [Berry, 20]

What was once considered free time—that time spent away from the subjection of the workplace—is now assessed, packaged, individualized, to meet one's particular needs and sold by specialists as "sanity compensation exercises" for the imprisoned body. Mutual care, generosity, neighborliness, festivity, communal joy—all the qualities that emerge with cooperative growing, nurturing, and harvesting of food—are smashed beneath the overshadowing gears of the machine and the dulled consciousness of humanity. Sociality is bent, mutilated, and spindled beneath the wheels of one-dimensional, competitive, or distributive progress. Participation in life means abstention from life!

The loss of personal freedom that come from this departure

from our primitive ancestors has not been problematic for most social theorists writing today; they have not concluded that social progress is non-existent or a non-reality. This is the case because it is no longer thought that each person's need to search for and create meaning, understanding, and solidarity rests in each person's freedom. It is believed to rest in the power of the state and professional expertise, the state's ability to manage well, to allocate freedom equally. Mutual aid or mutual support, a necessary condition for freedom, for being that self which one truly is, has been inverted to mean support for and support by state and professional expertise.

The days of most Americans who shout about free enterprise or the coming progress under a socialized existence are empty of life and hope. All things to them are utilitarian, pragmatic, commodities to be used, lacking the beauty to stir our dreams. "A day without such contacts and emotional stirrings—responses to the perfume of a flower or an herb, to the flight or the song of a bird, to the flash of a human smile or the warm touch of a human hand—that is, a day such as millions spend in factories, in offices, on the highway, is a day empty of organic contents and human rewards" (Mumford, 1970:383).

State communism, state socialism or planned capitalism, despite their ideological claims to foster sociality or progress, provide little in the way of restoring our severed partnership with nature, in fact seem to minimize the importance of personal freedom and sociability as much as multinational capitalism does. Consciousness is created that the free individual can contribute little and that he or she depends for personal well—being upon the activities of everyone (past, present, future) and party elites. Human needs as the material for shared responsibility for life are transformed into human needs as political irresponsibility, political deficiency. Human needs and natural dependency are regarded as counter-revolutionary, a drain on the revolutionary state. Diversity, uniqueness, though these qualities might be the essence of what it means to be human, are treated as counter-revolutionary.

In state-directed, state-supported economies human partnership with nature is equally minimized. The movements of nature are controlled not for the profit of corporate elites but for state bureaucracy elites. Human intimacy with nature is also feared by state-directed economies, for its organic anarchy, its flourishing interdependence, is a threat to the political-economic principles of the state. So people are desperately shielded from the importance of reading nature, for in the environment

there are no constitutions or hierarchies, no officials, no roles (that world is not a state), no schedules, no duties—though there are imperative loyalties requiring the mother tirelessly to feed her young, the mate to defend the bower, the species to maintain itself, even by stratagems as destructive to individuals as lemming migration. [Jerome, 270]

The mystery, the mutual arising, the growing, dying, and resurrection processes in nature speak against mechanical, political progress and the one-dimensional notions of freedom and human experience that come with party politics. Dialectically, nature affirms that pleasure is not possible without pain, wealth is not possible without poverty, health is not possible without sickness, progress without destruction, political hierarchy and sameness without death to the entire village.

Increasingly people of all nations condition themselves to unlearn and discard all the lessons of cooperation and interdependence transmitted by our ancestors. We stand by as species of whales, birds, elephants, populations of people, parts of the food chain are systematically depleted and deleted. We stand by as natural growth processes are increasingly twisted to fit the efficiency specifications of the machine. One simple example is the geometrification of the tomato which agrifacturers have attempted to grow to uniform size and to ripen at the same time in order that crops of tomatoes might be harvested by an automatic picking and packing machine. Another is the injection of livestock with chemically filled fattening needles and the caging of poultry into sunless houses to produce protein-deficient eggs.

Elimination and waste production now make taking time unprofitable. Waste products are now marketed; they are no longer by-products that are returned to the soil for its rejuvenation. The cycle of growth and decay is split and simultaneously the life-supporting sentiments that accompany familiarity with these natural processes disappear from our consciousness. Nature is blocked out like the pattern for a tailored suit; everything is cut to size, customized, and atomized to fit the construction specifications of a technological mentality. We become further removed from our history and origins. We therefore sever ourselves from any future of cooperative work. We attempt to protect our future with new industrial wares and planned competitions and nuclear power, but without a reading of who we are, why we are here.

For those who keep arguing for practical tools, I would assert that to read nature is the first step in putting in our hands a tool for survival, for reducing the violence that permeates our existence, and for insuring personal safety in the village. There are many who have come to recognize the importance of this already. As each of us moves toward oneness with our environment by cooperative living in that environment, we become more in touch with our natural competencies, for we get in touch with our needs. To read nature is our present economic and social necessity.

This literacy tool is not forged in the steel furnaces of the megamachine or within the hierarchical chamber of capitalist or socialist bureaus but through our hands. Through the application of our hands to the soil, our souls speak to us about what the universe is, about who we are both individually and collectively. Dialectically, our dreams and visions will emerge only with the sociality that comes from the sweat lining our brow, from our hardened hands cleansed by the soil of the earth.

People speak of environmental concerns in terms of an ecology move-ment or energy conservation movement, but these social movements only add to our already distorted concept of partnership with nature. They are movements which the economy of capitalism itself can contain and even profit from and therefore allow, much like welfare rights, civil rights, worker rights, and women's rights movements (Piven and Cloward). The very language reflects the severed partnership where nature is treated as something outside us. Our language reflects the lack of a more funda-mental understanding that

we and our country create one another, are literally part of one another; that our land passes in and out of our bodies just as our bodies pass in and out of our land; that as we and our land are part of one another, so all who are living as neighbors here, human and plant and animal, are part of one another, and so cannot possibly flourish alone; that therefore, our culture must be our response to our place, our culture and our places images of each other and inseparable from each other, and so neither can be better than the other. [Berry, 22]

To harm what we term other, whether it be a person or species, is to harm one's own self. When Cain kills and exploits Abel, he also kills and exploits himself, for he destroys the very community that enables him to be free. To imprison one flower is to imprison our entire food chain; to cage one human is to cage the souls of all humanity.

If our speech has been lacking the syntax to illustrate the unity that exists in the universe, it is because we have not lived cooperatively to create the words. The speech is not part of our conscious, living lives. Humankind vs nature, or person vs environment, is not in fact an adequate category for expressing the duality that exists between ourselves and that which is outside ourselves. While we have to select pairs of words in order to understand and describe unity, we cannot begin with the very words that imply or get their definition from the hierarchical relationships be-tween ourselves and our natural surroundings, where the human is central or the pinnacle of life, and then expect to find an avenue toward under-standing unity. To begin with language that serves the needs of political hierarchy is to end with that hierarchy and all its consequences, namely, the domination, exploitation, and violation of each other, what we have been trying to correct all along. In Eastern philosophy, for example, the Tao expresses the natural unity of things, but in the West we have not had such a concept before Aristotle (Moran, 135–48).

Clearly, abolishing capitalism or the state, prisons or professions, so that the working class or the poor or the disadvantaged can receive the full fruits of their labors, so that the individual worker can receive the whole product of his or her labor, will not bring about an end to existing hierarchical relations and presently existing divisions. This kind of thinking denies the vast heritage of installations built by people in the past, the accumulated techniques and traditions of civilization, our past cooperative relationship to nature and in work. It denies the collective, cooperative roots of our humanity that have brought us this far.

We must begin to think of the word "nature" as referring to the experienced whole of reality, all that is. We then can proceed to investigate the relation between the human and non-human, the personal and non-personal, the living and non-living, the healthy and the sick, insofar as these relations characterize the whole and each thing in it. We can begin to grasp that the "we" and the "other" are not separable things but go along with each other in partnership. In terms of human acts, we can begin to grasp that the good and the bad, the criminal and the non-criminal, are not separable things, but go along with each other in partnership. It is the bad, the criminal, the sick that is our material for growth and creation as a community evolving with a purpose.

24

MUTUAL AID MEDICINE

Restoration between Hands and Soil

The practical effects of our severed partnership with nature are particularly evident in the changing nature of the self-sufficient household. If we look at the changes that have taken place in the preparation of food—that is, our relationship to the soil as a community—we can understand better our changing relations in families and households, the household reflecting a particular kind of family. We see from history that the more communities and individuals have moved away from a subsistence economy, based on the kindly use of the land—through which they satisfy their own needs with their own hands—the more life has moved toward a commodity, professionalized existence, the more support there has been for the control, privatization, and further exploitation of natural resources. This historical departure from social progress has come full circle in the present politicization of food and natural resources. This is the sickness we face.

At one time, through the kindly use of the land, those who lived together in the household and village community were grounded in the soil and through this grounding were joined to each other in mutual aid. Peter Kropotkin spent a lifetime in studying this relationship, discovering that communities and groups that lost sight of this intimate relationship to the earth also lost sight of their relationship to each other and began to undergo social decay. Social epidemics emerged. There is a profound mutuality between land-soil-farm and household, between the production of food or work on the self-sufficient farm and social health in the entire community. Economics had its roots in the management of social relations in the household where people were instilled with the principle that "it is impossible to care for each other more or less differently than we care for the earth. . . .The earth is what we all have in common, it is what we are made of and what we live from. . . we therefore cannot damage it without damaging those with whom we share it" (Berry, 123-24).

This relationship or partnership with the soil is not unlike the relationship of people with plants and animals discussed in the previous section. The basic principle is the same, whereby intimate knowledge of the source of food influences sociability within the household, among households, between farm and town, farm and city. The idea of self-sufficient farm, on which the farmer lived, always included the idea of a household, a sharing community. An integral part of the farm's economy was the economy of its household as well as that of the village surrounding it, for the farm also helped to feed other households in towns and cities. But the households were not ensconced in a passive, commodity-based existence, as Wendell Berry notes:

These households were dependent on the farms, but not passively so, for their dependence was limited in two ways. For one thing, the town or city household was itself often a producer of food: at one time town and city lots routinely included garden space and often included pens and buildings to accommodate milk cows, fattening hogs, and flocks of poultry. For another thing, the urban household carefully selected and prepared the food that it bought; the neighborhood shops were suppliers of kitchen raw materials to local households, of whose needs and tastes the shopkeepers had personal knowledge. The shopkeepers were under the direct influence and discipline of their customers' wants, which they had to supply honestly if they hoped to prosper. The household was therefore not merely a unit in the economy of food production; its members practiced essential productive skills. The consumers of food were also producers or processors of food. [31]

Even as far back as the feudal period, people were collectively bound together on the land, to the point of shared responsibility for human needs, including shared responsibility for social harms. There was an intense feeling of belonging to a place, a clan, but one that went far beyond one's immediate family or ancestral relations. Though land was differentially owned, it was mutually shared; there was no such thing as exclusive property rights, whereupon a land "owner" could sell land in a market as a parcel of property. While it might be difficult to imagine, privatization was as foreign a concept as it is familiar to us today. Everyone had a place in the clan, everyone was related in the household, so there was no need to define relationship in terms of property. As Block suggests:

The tenant who—from father to son, as a rule—ploughs the land and gathers in the crop; his immediate lord, to whom he pays dues and who, in certain circumstances, can resume permission of the land; the lord of the land, and so on right up the feudal scale—how many persons there are so can say, each with (equal) justification. . ., "This is my field!" [Kennedy]

From the end of feudalism on, those who were pushed from the collective household to an individualized wage existence developed a different sense of responsibility moving from an ethic of shared responsibility to an ethic of individualistic responsibility. The productive relationship to the soil, that all shared at one time, was modified into a productive relationship to the bodies of others, the exiles from the land, that a few profited from.

We began to see nothing wrong with putting the body—most often somebody else's body, but frequently our own—to a task that insulted the mind and demeaned the spirit. And we began to find it easier than ever to prefer our own bodies to the bodies of other creatures and to abuse, exploit and otherwise hold in contempt those other bodies for the greater good or comfort of our own. [Berry, 104]

Cooperative work as well as cooperative acceptance of human misery was modified to meet the new ethic "to each according to his or her works" by which those who profited most from the works of individualized workers assumed the whole cooperative tradition for themselves. The collective tradition passed from the consciousness of those being enslaved by wages. The expertise that came with that tradition increasingly came within the domain of professional elites, which the disenfranchised exile had to pay for in order to reap its benefits. The feeling of solidarity, of belonging to a place, to a household of kindred, who shared responsibility for needs which often went beyond one's immediate specialized world, disappeared. Nor were the traditional ceremonies and festivities left to remind people of their collective heritage. It certainly was and is not taught in the state-certifying schools, for the tradition of collective responsibility for life denies certification of the individual. With the unitization of the land (private property) came the unitization of social relations and our present village of strangers. Away from the anarchy of the soil, the seasons, the mutual aid context of the self-sufficient household, the body was increasingly forced into the enslaving patterns of a managed, commodity-based existence. And it is critical to notice over time the changing role given to the body, for it is with the body, its hands, that the soil is grasped and understood in both its productive and mystical components. It is in the body, through hands, where health resides. The human body is increasingly seen only as a profitable energy source, an extension of a megamachine owned by elites, to be valued not in terms of its needs or sociality but in terms of time-motion, its ability to produce. "It was no longer a question of treating the body, enmasse, 'wholesale,' as if it were an indissociable unity, but of working it 'retail,' individually; or exercising upon it at the level of the mechanism itself—movements, gestures, attitudes, rapidity. . ." (Foucault, 1977:137).

The result of the privatizing of land and the enslavement of the body away from the soil is that the household is now simply a house or residence, a unit of consumption where the enslaved bodies heal themselves. The ethic among its members is one of competition rather than cooperation. In its nuclearized form all members desire to escape (e.g., wife-mother, children), even the prevailing power-based manager—the male. As the self-sufficient farm has ceased to be a place to live, a place to die, to learn and give birth, as it has become a factory, a corporate unit of production, the collaborative relationship that once existed between farm and household, between soil and body, among family members, between households, has become increasingly extinct. It has been replaced by competitive, self-interest relations. "Healthy homes are transformed into hygienic apartments where one cannot be born, cannot be sick, and cannot die decently. Not only are helpful neighbors a vanishing species, but also liberal doctors who make house calls" (Illich, 1978:34). All the bonds of union among the residents of the same street or neighborhood have all but dissolved. It is no surprise that community residents clamor against correctional group homes and halfway houses, for they fear being taken over by the very problems economic progress promised sanctuary from. So shaky are the social bonds of the neighborhood that residents are not able to accommodate to any possible alternate reality, particularly a reality that represents criminal or insane elements. And the more families and communities become competitive, nuclearized, "wardized," the more support they require from the state and professional experts.

And whereas once the local merchant was only a supplier of raw materials to the community—a good year was defined according to how little one had to purchase from the merchant—the producers and regulators of goods now have an investment in the social relations of the family, its consumption rates, its management, and the identities of its members. The merchant, another among the professions competing for clients, has taken on many of the traditional functions of household members and the self-sufficient farm, becoming increasingly both processor and producer for the disintegrating household and its helpless members. The merchant has become a kind of arch-executive of the family and household, watching over the consumption patterns of household members (by market research), producing and providing food and even means of sociability, all offered for profit. What all develop—both consumers and producers—is a careless attitude about everything, except the satisfaction of one's addictions.

What distinguishes the modern family residence from the household is the web of dependence on commodities and experts as the source of sociality. The forms of partnership that subsistence economy encourages among members has disappeared. "To satisfy this dependence, more of the same must be produced; standardized, engineered goods, designed for the future consumer who will be trained by the engineer's agent to need what he or she is offered" (Illich, 1977:6).

At the same time the state and its certifying professions become arch-executives over our safety and sanity needs, producing sociality and regulating partnerships for the addicted, helpless consumer. Whereas once quality of life was given meaning through personal taste, preference, good husbandry, and sociality, its meaning is now defined by the centralized home-office standards of professionalized merchants and the state, standards that, as our economy becomes internationally based, become merely political-economic tools for triage compliance. The inevitable has come true, where quality of life is now defined by all things external to nature and human needs—cheapness, convenience, efficiency. The standards of the good life have changed from those based on the degree of lived freedom to those based on salability, quotas and rations, without regard for harm to people, land and the natural balance of things. This is the sickness we require medicine for.

Our ethics and feelings of solidarity are no longer grounded in connectedness to or partnership with the land. Therefore, these communal festivities that celebrate life and our participation in it have been replaced by seasonal consumption periods (e.g., Christmas), by managerial rituals, bureaucratic procedure, the therapeutic hour. Bigness, centralization, unitization, thwart the healthy culture, the partnered, connected culture which has "a communal order of memory, insight, value, work, conviviality, reverence, aspiration. It reveals the human necessities and human limits. It clarifies our inseparable bonds to the earth and to each other. It assures that the necessary restraints are observed, that the necessary work is done, and that it is done well" (Berry, 43).

The consumer-commodity orientation is now an international issue. As commodity experts attempt to adjust people's needs for the sake of profit, so political experts are attempting to adjust population size internationally by rationing food, oil, wood, natural gas. Social good is said to result from rational coordination, from management, and from politically based food chains designed by mandarins. And it seems that a person will eat or warm him or herself in proportion to how he or she fits into and gives loyalty to international triage policy, or "planned capitalism." Economic allocations—food, oil, clothing—are made in accord with nation-state conformity standards. America's official policy on food, for example, as reflected in the statement of Earl Butz, former United States secretary of agriculture, is: "Food is a weapon!" Since warmaking is now unprofitable, given the multinationals' overlapping boundaries in nation states, maintenance war is now waged, a cold war of natural resources. Some people seem to sleep more easily thinking that the killing of people through starving and freezing them to death is more humane than napalming them. The irony is that the source of life—food—has come to be viewed as weaponry.

Dostoyevsky argued that "the degree of civilization in a society can be judged by entering its prisons." I agree, but I think there is a more comprehensive and more accurate measure—a society's regard for the body. A human is his or her body; the body is his or her situation, as Gabriel Marcel has noted. It is one's bridge to the world, a model of the world in which it is situated (Keen, 148). The treatment of the body of each in a culture is indicative of the quality of life in that culture. Whether we wish to call a person a bureaucrat, the organization person, the robopath or statecrat, we are witnessing the increasing imprisonment of the body societally, whereby people willingly consent to the repetition of labor, standardized acts, and a depersonalized schedule, devoid of any human value. The prison is only one limited form of this enslavement. It is one part of a mesmerized containment of the body whereby any officially sanctioned fantasy is employable, whether it actualized into the killings at Attica, My Lai, Dachau, Buchwald, or the present triage killing through the emerging lifeboat ethic. With the body imprisoned, there are new acts of violence, new administrative forms of violence, a new silent assent to slow destruction—and acts of terrorism in response. Acts of violence are carried out by orderly, obedient bodies in administratively safe and efficient ways. As Teilhard de Chardin noted: "The Big Brain thinks, therefore I am not." Violence that invades one's person through administrative procedure is not recognized as violence but as good administrative procedure.

All this has been accompanied by a dissatisfaction with the body as it naturally is for each person. As Berry states: "For the appropriate standard for the body—that is, health—has been replaced, not even by another standard but by very exclusive physical *models*" (112). People strive to meet ideal dimensions, with appropriate dimensions for the perfect man and perfect woman—clothed and unclothed, alone and together. The worst flaw is to begin to look old, for one begins to take on the qualities for which the future-based society no longer has a cure, only the perfect, consumer-based funeral, after which one is buried in a state-certified burial place. I am talking about the perfect consumer body where the unique forms and wrinkles that reflect one's individual relation to the world and others are hidden, discarded through programmed weight loss, programmed physical utopias—the spa.

Mechanical regularity prevails, devoid of all spontaneity, where "to follow the program, to obey instructions, to 'pass the buck,' to be uninvolved as a person in the needs of other person, to limit responses to what lies immediately, so to say on the desk, to heed no relevant human considerations, however vital: never to question the origin of an order or inquire as to its ultimate destination: to follow through every command, however irrational, to make no judgements of value or relevance about the work in hand, finally to eliminate feelings or emotions or rational moral misgivings that might interfere with the immediate dispatch of work." (Mumford, 1970:278). It is the person of fear, paranoia, boredom, powerlessness, who will buy or vote for or obey anything that is attractively packaged—exiles of the soil, of hands, of connectedness. This is the foundation of our culture today.

25

MUTUAL AID FAMILIES

Social Relations Based on Direct Action, Hospitality, and Free Agreement

If we have become a culture of violence and crime, of greed and exploitation, of eroding freedom, as the world emerges into a single economic order, we are beginning simultaneously to recognize what we are doing to each other. People are becoming increasingly aware of our mutual dependency as nations, as communities, as neighbors for the most basic things in life—food, oil, wood, companionship. We are becoming more conscious of the need to cooperate with each other if we are to survive. We see that what I have termed the state throughout this book is not some abstract identity outside ourselves, but each one of us in a particular kind of relationship to each other. As Gustav Landauer has commented: "The state is not something which can be destroyed by a revolution, but is a condition, a certain relationship between human beings, a mode of human behavior; we destroy it by contracting other relationships, by behaving differently" (Ward, 19).

This condition, this certain relationship, is one of power, hierarchy, punishment, and enslavement, where everyday life decisions about people are made by a few people at the top and sold in the form of commodities (political and industrial) to a broad base of people at the bottom. (Ward, 22). This is true for the state as profession where the expertise, information, and traditions that come from communal living over millennia are channeled off into certifying institutions where certifiers produce the next generations of certifiers. This privatized, elitist way of life I call the state is different from that in mutual aid arrangements, those based on direct action, families of hospitality, free agreement, and the principle of freedom as the basis for solidarity and justice.

The requirements of community lived according to the principles of mutual aid are first of all the rejection of professionalized, expert, institutionalized life for face-to-face living conditions. This means, as I noted above, direct action in our lives, that is, "action, which, in respect to the situation, realizes the end desired, so far as this lies within one's power or the power of one's group" (Wieck). I am talking about direct action for producing food, for education, for agreeable work, for healing. Only through direct action will a sense of justice based on the well-being of each materialize. While direct action as I have described it might be regarded by many as impractical for designing workable systems of change, it is in fact the only humanly secure and safe way to change. It is the only human way we know. Our history of creating systems and social hierarchies to support those systems proves this! Direct action is often rejected outright because it does not have the mammoth proportions that systems project, however futile and unrealizable those projections are and have been.

When we think about what we assume to be necessary and true, and start wondering about what else might be possible instead, we consciously change our day-to-day actions in ways that change the world we live in. And this adds up, we see that we take a different world for granted and that other things now appear sensible and possible to us. [Fischer, 1978:15]

No matter how global one's concerns are, no matter how compassionate a person is, a person can live fully in this world with others only by living responsibly in one small part of it. Goals that are global and infinitely remote are not goals at all, but deceptions. For those interested in solving what is advertised as the crime problem, I contend that direct action in their own lives is the first step; it is our only means for safety as a community.

Within a mutual aid framework direct action corrections does not mean attempting to rectify harmful or hurtful behavior after the fact, according to abstract standards of right and wrong, but entails establishing a human social context in which all the acts, feelings, aspirations, and hurts of persons struggling to be human are resolved on a face-to-face basis, cooperatively—before, while, and after people are hurt. I am talking about a new sense of family or community. Whether one chooses to call it intentional family, or intentional community, or affinity group, I am referring to human relationships based on an ethic of shared responsibility for life, for each other's needs despite a person's particular merits, works, or economic fluidity. In whatever form the community takes, it is community based on shared aspirations, in which each person desires (1) to know the other as part of one's shared present, but also as reflecting a different, unique reality; (2) to meet the other's needs; and (3) to lean on the other for moral support on occasions where it is deemed necessary. I am talking about developing social conditions in which no one person's expression requires the enforced activity of another, but rather where each person is encouraged to develop self-sufficient tools and self-certified competencies. In terms of education, this means apprenticeships of some sort; in terms of health, this means healing at home, being insane in the community, giving birth at home; in terms of work, it entails worker definition of the means and end uses of what is produced or contemplated.

To try to grow, to find meaning, to heal the body and the soul, in isolation and without mutually supportive relations is to collaborate in the continuing severing of body from soul, your needs from mine, age group from age group, race from race. Healing is impossible in the isolation of power-based relations, in acts that reinforce isolation and severing. Healing is the opposite of power and isolation. Healing is conviviality and hospitality, is mutual aid.

In mutual aid communities social relations are based on hospitality rather than hostility. Community or family must become a free space, as it were, where each of us struggling with his or her own estrangement, physical and emotional, can find support for who we are. Community or family is not relationship for the purpose of changing or transforming others, for normalizing or disciplining them, but an offering of human presence, a place where change can take place freely. "It is not to bring men and women over to our side, but to offer freedom not disturbed by dividing lines" (Nouwen, 51), whether these dividing lines be those of sex, age, race, or income. "It is not to lead our neighbor into a corner where there are no alternatives left, but to open a wide spectrum of options for choice and commitment." As people begin to open themselves up to the possibility of cooperation in work and play, they begin to "discover that it is *not* devastating to accept the positive feeling of another, that is does not necessarily end in hurt, that it actually 'feels good' to have another person with you in your struggles to meet life—this may be one of the most profound lessons encountered by the individual whether in therapy or not" (Rogers, 1961:85).

The paradox of hospitality or conviviality "is that it wants to create emptiness, not a fearful emptiness, but a friendly emptiness where strangers can enter and discover themselves as created free, free to sing their own songs, speak their own language, dance their own dances; free also to leave and follow their vocations" (Nouwen, 51) at whatever age they choose. If individuals wish to resolve their differences by no longer holding on to past contracts, then so be it. Human relationships are ever-negotiable, impermanent, and dependent upon free agreement or voluntary commitment. Punishment and power do not foster commitment but rather destroy this urge to commit oneself to a life's work and to another. There can be no commitment to another person or a life's work unless one is free to express and engage one's own needs in the journey of life as these needs unfold. There is no time or place or age group, or race or sex or class, to which this unfolding or revelation is especially limited. It cannot, therefore, be standardized, as it has been within capitalist and state communist societies through law and decree. What does not vary is the necessity for each person to exist in the world, to be at work there, to be there in the midst of other people, and to be mortal there (Sartre, 38).

The resolution of hurts that emerge among people is based on a collective or shared responsibility for the acts of each person, for we all share in the work and setbacks, the health and sickness of each other. Resolution takes place in the spirit that all possible circumstances had not theretofore been fully explored, emotions not fully expressed, and needs not fully satisfied. The conflicts and confusion that hurts produce are resolved humanly only when we understand their interpersonal or interactional precedents. Conflicts emerge not because people strive to deny meaning in their lives, but because they seek it so dearly. When differences are discussed in their social context, the existential meaning of participants can be understood. The meaning that participants give to the situation must be understood, for only then can the reality of cultural diversity and human authenticity exist. Every theory and form of practice "which takes man out of the moment in which he becomes aware of himself is, at the very beginning a theory which confounds truth" (Sartre, 36).

I am talking about face-to-face justice or corrections in which all the complexities that accompany differences or hurts are aired, all the hurts both real and imagined, the angers, the rage, the full range of human emotions that persist. This involves full receptivity to each person's "story" from that person's point of view. It entails seeing how it feels to him or her, sensing his or her frame of reference. The story may be hard to tell, hard to listen to, full of human "disappointments, *but it is the only story the stranger has*, because *it is his own* and there will be no hope for the future when the past remains unconfessed, unreceived and misunderstood" (Nouwen, 68).

While this may sound to many like a tortuous route, there is no other way of making contact with another human being, of creating the conditions of solidarity. Walls, punishment, imposed schedules, therapies based on power, not the well being of each, will not do. They never have. Despite Hobbes, Skinner, Wilson, and Van den Haag, and the seeming endless list of those who support punishment and power-based relations, the history of the human community tells us otherwise. It tells us that punishment and power destroy, and that when they persist as social evolutionary means the group decays and soon passes out of existence.

People who have hurt others, especially those who have hurt others seriously, are people whose needs have not been met, whose stories have not been told, and who limit themselves foolishly to power and enforcement as means to satisfy their needs, which, once denied as valid, become demons to be unleashed upon the world. Only a mutual aid milieu will help to satisfy these human needs humanly and foster the dissolution of power, highlighting its utter insanity. All that each of us can do for another is "to wait and watch and listen patiently, to keep our hands off, to refrain from being too active and brusque, too interfering and controlling, and most important of all in trying to understand another person—to keep our mouths shut and our ears and eyes wide open" (Maslow, 13). If you poke at people, manipulate them toward some a priori established schedule of life that is not theirs, and take them apart for profit or ideology, they will disintegrate before your eyes as persons. They will become or remain distrustful of the process that provides hope. Their view of people and the world as untrustworthy and unrewarding will be reinforced and offer another justification for keeping themselves hidden and abstaining from sharing in their own struggle to be human. They will deem their inner selves, their feelings and needs, to be insane, too complex for the standardized power system pressing upon them. They will come to see power as the only way to resolve or dissolve the driving needs of their suspect selves, in a suspect world. It is critical to remember that "trust and hope don't cause healing. They *are* healing" (Jourard, 68). The presence of trust and hope is an indication that the conditions of life are present.

The power to heal or correct or restore what has been severed comes through the sharing of presence, which each of us has to offer. This presence is not something that exists solely in the expert's office or education credentials or managerial style but it exists within each of us and is passed on within the collective traditions of humankind. There is no human justification, therefore, for denying personal responsibility for creating community by passing off responsibility to expert committees or bureaucratic task forces. No special or permanent personages, languages, or offices are needed to create community. These in fact must compete with and destroy presence for their own continuation. The resolution of conflicts or differences, the satisfaction of new and old needs, cannot be achieved in a professional theater where the drama is geared toward winning an audience over to one's side, for there are no sides. The resolution process is a forum for the revelation of self, one's needs as they exist in the present situation. It is a forum for creating new consciousness about community, and new consciousness is created only when there is shared responsibility for living together. Each person and community as a whole can begin to reevaluate what is possible for binding each other together in the future. Present cooperative struggle breeds hope.

The resolution of hurts and differences in a mutual aid context always involves returning to work and living with the other(s) in community, with a new sense of work, relationship, needs and hope. Clearly, this differs from state-professional corrections, where conflicts are thought of as zero-sum situations, one claim superior, the other inferior to appropriate, one winner, one loser. (Tifft, 1979), where those who "lose" are isolated in state institutional containers, where they isolate themselves further from emotional involvement with others, as a means of survival. They begin a movement away from the very conditions that heal or make whole. If any standard of community or justice can be set, it must be based on "whether the spirit—the You, saying, responding spirit—remains alive and actual; whether what remains of it in communal life continues to be subjected to the state and the economy or whether it becomes independently active; whether what abides of it in individual human life incorporates itself again in communal life" (Buber, 1958). Human experience, experiencing humanly in the present, in the presence of others, can be the only established criterion, for only thus do individuals and groups evolve successfully.

Resolutions of conflict in the context of mutual aid do not end in hatred, for the foundations of that hatred are explored and given vent and changed, perhaps by people doing more agreeable work—a revolutionary idea for this culture! These kinds of resolutions can only evolve into a deeper commitment on the part of people to each other, to community living. The conflicts themselves are seen as the material for growth and solidarity. Done through face-to-face negotiation, instead of through an impersonal, stigmatizing system, such resolutions bring each person to trust more in others. People trust more of what is other in themselves and to accept what is unique and different in others. This has both social and religious consequences, for the exiled, fugitive deities that inhabit the woods and streams and fields can be welcomed to our receptive consciousness; they are no longer seen as elements that are destructive to sanity or religion but as a positive foundation for both. Even each person's own unique, daimonic mystery, that will not allow rational control or understanding, is increasingly accepted.

Bit by bit each person finds him or herself rejecting power and punishment as methods for correcting severed relationship, realizing that such processes destroy the foundations of personal history, and of personal and communal continuity. They destroy presence and therefore the essence of history, the struggling, vulnerable self in the community. One experiences a dying to methods that reinforce a life based on status and differentiation, that sever connectedness, that assert: "You are guilty.

I am innocent!" We find we can begin to forgo conceptions of life based on privatization and ethics, of "private property, whatever it is; our knowledge, our good name, our land, our money, or the many objects we have collected around us" (Nouwen, 73).

A life lived according to the principles of mutual aid also involves the recognition and continuing acceptance of our limitations as human beings, whether these limitations are referred to as mortality, scarcity, crime, hurts, needs. These are all elements that constitute human misery, that we inherit not because of things such as inefficient free enterprise but by virtue of the fact that we are mortal. They are forms of life that no amount of industrialized progress or state control can dispel. In our present culture, where the state and its certifying professions serve as novocaines to these painful aspects of our living together, we have lost touch with the sense that part of the human condition is the dreadful pain of loss and that in many situations all that is humanly possible for "correcting" the misery is to accept it, to accept the pain of our own helplessness and powerlessness as part of our life together, and to forgive.

Recognizing, accepting, and living with the pain of hurts, scarcity, recurring needs, with the fact that each of us will die, that people hurt one another, oftentimes senselessly is a condition of human growth and fulfillment. It is a prerequisite to communal solidarity. Only by coming to grips with this facet of our humanity can we come to reach out and cooperate with others. Lack or loss, however defined, is no longer seen solely as an unavoidable, resented concomitant to our living together, one that destroys progress, but as the material for progress. All aspects of life become urgent invitations to a response, to personal engagement, to connection with our own inner resources, and to cooperative engagement with others. What is now defined as negative, as life interruption in a profit-based economy, in fact can be seen as opportunities and challenges to an inner response to create.

The healing, sociability, and solidarity that mutual aid fosters is not without historical precedent, as the peasants of the small Belgian village of Gheel demonstrated. They said: 'Send us your insane. We will give them absolute freedom.' They adopted them into their families, gave them places at their tables, the chance alongside them to cultivate their fields, and a place among their young at their country balls. 'Eat, drink, and dance with us. Work, run about the fields and be free.' That was the system that was all the science the Belgian peasant had. And liberty worked a miracle. The insane became cured. Even those who had incurable, organic lesions became sweet, tractable members of the family like the rest. The diseased mind would always work in an abnormal fashion but the heart was in the right place." (Kropotkin, 1968a:234). While this kind of hospitality was characteristic of much of the life in early colonial America, it has disappeared in the face of professionaldom. The Catholic Worker Movement in America is a current example of people willing to live cooperatively with those in need, to meet their needs without expectation that they must be other than who they are (William Miller). It is one of the few examples of mutual aid without the assistance of the state, where life to heal the sick is no different from life to support the well!

The irony in the history of state-professional corrections is that it is a continuing series of attempts to construct mutual aid communities, but as masks of love and caring. I am not talking here about people's intentions or motives or the sincerity of their concern for others: but about the structural conditions, the relational distance that is established and maintained by an indirect, bureaucratic structure for life. The efforts of people like Maxwell Jones (1953), all the forms of group-based treatment, the whole genre of community corrections, Synanon, Alcoholics Anonymous, are all attempts to imitate this mutual aid context. That they must isolate and take away our hurting members from the community into segregated units is the problem with them. The person in difficulty is treated as if he or she were somehow an aberration from life. The critical element that destroys the mutual aid and its ensuing freedom is the state-professional management that operates the milieu *from the outside*. A mask of love is used as a substitute for direct, face-to-face living together. The mask becomes a necessity in the power-based world because facing a possible alternate reality directly, one that might exist among the insane or criminal element, seems too overwhelming for people who live amidst the fragility of power and punishment. Relational distance becomes a way to survive one's own hurting humanity.

As I mentioned earlier in the discussion of Jerome Miller's program for juveniles in Massachusetts, even when correctional guards were offered full pay by Jerome Miller to take into their homes one juvenile delinquent from the institutions that were being closed down, they refused! Was their addiction to the mask of love so great? They preferred to report to work in an empty institution and sit idly, doing their own time without the state-assigned raison d'être for being there. Had the guards, in effect, become the inmates, the new state clientele!

Mutual aid involves a commitment on the part of each person to be free. Without individual freedom as the foundation stone for living together, there can be no justice. Justice before the law has come to mean equalization of escape, certified escape from the red tape that reduces the rate of consuming. When I say that justice is freedom, I do not mean a freedom exempt from pain, hurts, suffering, but the recognition and acceptance of these as part of living together. I am not talking about a crime-free, insanity-free society, a free-wheeling, painless utopia, but life as it is, with its deaths, hurts, and joys, and then life as it might be to survive our hardships.

All else entails serving the mandates of a system of power and those who live through power-based relations. To be free is to assent to the basic goodness and perfectibility of each person, on the one hand, but simultaneously to recognize and accept their ever-present fragility on the other. But it is mutual aid directly applied, not the shadowing walls of prisons and helpers, that fosters restoration of wholeness and solidarity.

Freedom, then, is not some kind of movement toward a superior independence, a political aloofness or point in one's life where one can escape all that is inferior, all that one cannot control or possess. No person can be self-determining and independent, without mutually supportive relationships. Without the latter all movement toward independence is simply movement toward new forms of isolation. Accepted dependence brings freedom, for through its recognition as a part of independence and through expression of its presence comes the understanding that one is not alone in life, that one can share with and be receptive to another without being annihilated or having to control all the time to survive safely. We have a basic desire to be dependent, "the wish to share responsibility for the control of one's impulses and the direction of one's life" (Slater, 5), for both impulses and the tools for directing them are social as well as personal. In our present culture these impulses are seen as the cause of insanity and harm, so we avoid them, deny their force in our lives, thereby creating and confirming the very condition that bring forth both.

In the hierarchical social arrangements we struggle in now, supported only by tenuous power, our movement toward freedom is continually thwarted by the twentieth-century disease of the "disordered will," a desire to control the uncontrollable, to will or produce health, sanity, correctedness, to think that it is possible to deal with everything unpleasant through novocaines and avoidance routines, to will things into and out of reality because they are painful or hurtful or sinful or simply different. But this does not foster human well being and solidarity, connectedness, or continued partnerships either within the universe of nature or among people. We cannot will or produce what is the essence of our humanity, our freedom: "I can will knowledge, but not wisdom; going to bed, but not sleeping; eating, but not hunger; meekness, but not humility; scrupolosity, but not virtue; self-assertion or bravado, but not sympathy; congratulations, but not admiration; religiosity, but not faith; reading, but not understanding" (Farber).

Similarly, it is not possible to will art, music, or anything that reflects creativity or growth. We cannot will our children or those temporarily dependent into some other form of humanity than that which they choose to take. The essence of creativity and growth, transformation and renewal, requires an abandonment of self to the present, subject to the fluid and competing demands of an uncontrollable present. Keats, unlike Marx, understood this, a state of being he described as "negative capability": that is, when man is capable of being in uncertainties, mysteries, doubts, without any irritable reachings after fact and reason. It is to live without having to resolve everything with the finality, immediacy, and predictability required by economies of profit and state redistribution (Olson, 1970:14).

This movement toward the freedom to live cooperatively with others is a frightening responsible freedom and an individual moves toward it "cautiously, fearfully and with almost no confidence at first" (Rogers, 1961). For some people this movement is experienced as an overwhelming burden, so that they prefer to remain controlled, submissive, regulated, and subject to the will of others. As Colin Wilson states: "Freedom is the greatest burden of all; to tell everyman to think for himself, to solve the problem of good and evil and then act according to this solution: to live for truth and not for country or society, or his family" (1956:185). Many begin upon the journey but abandon it, unwilling to accept confrontation with a power-centered self, but what they soon discover is that, once begun, the process is irreversible. The only choice is greater freedom or new, more intense forms of slavery, more encapsulating than the old, for they are forms of slavery built on new forms of treason to self. This is not a new or old realism but eternal realism, bound not by ideology or race or sex or age but by freedom.

Zablocki describes the darkness and uncertainty and painful struggle with self of one person attempting to let go in her attempt to become part of a community:

I had to jump over this cliff and there was this chasm to get to where the people in the Bruderhof were. And I couldn't jump. I absolutely couldn't. I couldn't let go. I said to myself: "What the hell am I holding on to? I am holding on to this stupid, impoverished ego." I knew it, and I still couldn't do it. So there you are. To be able to let go, this is called faith—to believe in the impossible, to go ahead. [262-63]

The revolution of becoming free is not an event but a permanent and ongoing process. In this permanent revolution reformation "is vision, is spontaneity, perpetually renewed: everyday the last day, or the first day, the beginning and the end" (Brown, 235). It is foolish therefore to struggle to get some educational level, some emotional or spiritual state, or some economic level, to some level of certified state existence, for there is no social structure, no personage that will resolve all contradictions. The possibility of holiness, of wholeness is everywhere and eternal, and found in a present lived presently with others. We soon experience that "everything is holy. There is no special time or place or person, privileged to represent the rest. . . . The many are made only when the totality is in every part" (Brown, 239).

Once a free life is opted for, people begin to see the utter futility of structures imposed from the outside upon experience. The futility of political institutions for human change becomes apparent. The free person sees political organization for what it is: as theater, theatrical structure that *specializes*, that says some persons have special status and therefore deserve to take charge of and control other persons. Political revolution is simply organizational turnover, a turnover of metaphysical symbols, without any regard for the physics of life on which political systems derive their meaning. The free person recognizes that there is an infinite variety and number of social structures, resulting from each relationship that each person forms with any other, with the land, the soil, the universe. Accepting this fact, each of us can begin to take charge of his or her own life and become part of history, for each person is in reality its creator, not its slave.

Freedom, then, comes with continuing movement toward the full engagement of life, toward partnership with others. It is not simply a "freedom from," an opting out of society or an escape from ourselves. Freedom is a "freedom to" as well, a movement to renew connections, to heal the severed partnerships between body and mind, work and play, male and female, young and old, body and earth. It is present and active participation in life. I am talking about

a society in which all the mutual relations of its members are regulated, not by laws, not by authorities, whether self-imposed or elected, but by mutual agreements, between the members of the society, and by a sum of social customs and habits—not pertrified by law, routine or superstition, but continually developing and continually readjusted in accordance with the ever-growing requirements of a free life. [Kropotkin, 1968:157].

There is movement toward the dissolution of power as a means, the discarding of all forms of love's masks, to bring forth the eternally flowing love we carry for each other in our presence freely given.

REFERENCES

Arendt, Hannah
  1958   *The Human Condition.* Chicago: University of Chicago Press.
  1978   Interview conducted by Roger Errera. *New York Review of Books* 25 (October 26): 18.
Banfield, Edward
  1972   *The Unheavenly City: The Nature and Future of the Urban Crisis.* Boston: Little, Brown.
Barkdull, Walter L.
  1976   "Probation: Call It Control and Mean It." *Federal Probation* 40 (December): 3–8.
Barnet, Richard J.
  1978   "No Room in the Lifeboats." *New York Times Magazine,* April 16 pp. 33–34.
Bellah, Robert
  1970   *Beyond Belief: Essays on Religion in a Post-Traditional World.* New York: Harper Row.
Bentham, Jeremy
  1843   *Works,* 4: 60–64. John Bowring, ed., 11 vols. (1838–43).
Berger, Bennet
  1971   "Child Rearing Practices of the Communal Family" Progress Report to NIMH. Mimeographed.
Berkman, Alexander
  1929   *Now and After: ABC of Communist Anarchism.* New York: Vanguard.
  1970   *Prison Memoirs of an Anarchist.* New York: Schocken.
Berrigan, Daniel
  1971   *No Bars to Manhood.* New York: Bantam.
Berry, Wendell
  1977   *The Unsettling of America.* San Francisco: Sierra Club.
Black, Donald
  1976   *The Behavior of Law.* New York: Academic Press.
Blackham, J. J. (ed.)
  1965   *Reality, Man and Existence: Essential Works of Existentialism.* New York: Bantam.
Brown, Norman O.
  1966   *Love's Body.* New York: Vintage.

Buber, Martin
1958   *Paths in Utopia.* Boston: Beacon.
1970   *I and Thou.* New York. Scribner's.
Cahn, Edgar, and Jean Cahn
1963   "The War on Poverty: A Civilian Perspective." *Yale Law Journal* 73:1317-53.
Cahn, Edmond
1966   *Confronting Justice.* Boston: Little, Brown.
Camus, Albert
1955   *The Myth of Sisyphus.* New York: Knopf.
Caplan, Arthur L. (ed.)
1978   *The Sociobiology Debate: Readings on Ethical and Scientific Issues.* New York: Harper Row.
Casper, Jonathan
1972   "Criminal Justice: The Consumer Perspective." U.S. Department of Justice. Washington, D.C. : U.S. Government Printing Office (February).
Chesler, Phyllis, and Emily Jane Goodman
1977   *Women, Money and Power.* New York: Bantam.
Christianson, Scott
1978a   "Corrections Law Developments: Prison Labor and Unionization– Legal Developments." *Criminal Law Bulletin* 14 (May-June): 243–47.
1978b   "Prisons, Prisons and More Prisoners." *Criminal Law Bulletin* 14 (March-April): 145–48.
1979a   "Execution by Lethal Injection." *Criminal Law Bulletin* 15 (January-February): 69–78.
1979b   "Storm over the Olympic Prison." *Criminal Law Bulletin* 15 (March-April) : 162–67.
Coughlin, Ellen K.
1978   "Radical Denied Tenure at U. of Maryland Branch." *Chronicle of Higher Education,* November 6, 1978.
Day, Dorothy
1972   *The Long Loneliness.* New York: Curtis.
Debs, Eugene
1927   *Walls and Bars.* Chicago: Socialist Party.
"Dr. Hutschnecker's Plan"
1970   *Newsweek,* April 20, pp. 76–77.
Duffee, David, and Robert Fitch
1976   *Introduction to Corrections: A Policy and Systems Approach.* Santa Monica: Goodyear.
Eiseley, Loren C.
1970   *The Invisible Pyramid.* New York: Scribner's.
Eliade, Mircea
1969   *The Quest: History and Meaning in Religion.* Chicago: University of Chicago Press.
Empey, LaMar T.
1967   *Alternatives to Incarceration.* Washington, D.C.: U.S. Government Printing Office.
Farber, Leslie H.
1968   *The Ways of the Will.* New York: Harper & Row.
Fischer, George
1976   "Anarchism As a Sociology: Lost and Found." Paper presented at the annual meeting of the American Sociological Association New York City (September 1).
1978   *Ways to Self Rule: Beyond Marxism and Anarchism.* New York: Vantage.
Fogel, David
1975   *We Are the Living Proof.* Cincinnati: W. H. Anderson.

Foucault, Michel
  1977   *Discipline and Punish*. New York: Pantheon.
Freud, Sigmund
  1948   *Group Psychology and the Analysis of Ego*. London: Hogarth.
  1963   "My Contact with Josef Popper-Lynkeus," in *Character and Culture*,
          trans. J. Strachey. New York: Crowell-Collier.
Fromm, Erich
  1976   *To Have or to Be?* New York: Harper & Row.
Goodman, Paul
  1952   *Utopian Essays and Practical Proposals*. New York: Vintage.
  1963   *People or Personnel*. New York: Random House.
  1977a   "Advance-Guard Writing in America, 1900–1950." pp. 144–64 in Taylor
          Stoehr, ed., *Creator Spirit Come!* New York: Free Life Editions.
  1977b   "An Apology for Literature." Pp. 267–84 in Taylor Stoehr ed., *Creator
          Spirit Come!* New York: Free Life Editions.
  1977c   "Notes on Neo-Functionalism." Pp. 48-54 in Taylor Stoehr ed., *Drawing
          the Line*. New York: Free Life Editions.
Gouldner, Alvin
  1971   *The Coming Crisis in Western Sociology*. New York: Avon.
Greenberg, David F.
  1977   "Fixed Sentencing: The Co-optation of a Radical Reform." Paper
          presented at the annual meeting of the American Society of Criminology
          (November), Atlanta.
Heilbroner, Robert L.
  1978a   "Boom and Crash." *New Yorker*, August 28, pp. 71–72.
  1978b   *Beyond Boom and Crash*. New York: Norton.
Heschel, Abraham
  1966   *The Insecurity of Freedom: Essays on Human Existence*. New York:
          Farrar, Straus & Giroux.
Hill, Judah
  1975   *Class Analysis: United States in the 1970s*. Emeryville, Calif.: Class
          Analysis.
Humboldt, Wilhelm Von
  1969   "The Limits of State Action" in J. W. Burrow ed., *Cambridge Studies in
          the History and Theory of Politics*. Cambridge: Cambridge University
          Press.
Huxley, Thomas H.
  1888   "The Struggle for Existence in Human Society." The *Nineteenth Century*
          23 (February) : 161–80.
Illich, Ivan
  1974   *Tools for Conviviality*. New York: Pantheon.
  1977   *Medical Nemesis: The Expropriation of Health*. New York: Bantam.
  1978   *Toward a History of Needs.* New York: Pantheon.
Instead of Prisons
  1976   *A Handbook for Abolitionists*. Prison Research Education Project,
          3049 E. Genesee St., Syracuse, New York.
Jerome, Judson
  1974   *Families of Eden: Communes and the New Anarchism*. New York:
          Seabury.
Jones, Maxwell
  1953   *The Therapeutic Community*. New York: Basic Books.
Jourard, Sidney
  1968   *Disclosing Man to Himself*. New York: Van Nostrand.
Kalecki, Michal
  1971   *Selected Essays on the Dynamics of the Capitalist Economy, 1933-1970*.
          New York: Cambridge.

Keen, Sam
1970   *To a Dancing God*. New York: Harper & Row.
Kennedy, Mark
1970   "Beyond Incrimination: Some Neglected Facets of the Theory of Punishment." *Catalyst* 5 (summer): 1-37.
Kierkegaard, Soren
1941   *The Sickness unto Death*. Princeton: Princeton University Press.
Kozol, Jonathan
1978   *Children of the Revolution*. New York: Delacorte.
Krisberg, Barry
1975   *Crime and Privilege*. Englewood Cliffs: Prentice-Hall.
Kropotkin, Peter
1902   *Mutual Aid: A Factor of Evolution*. New York: McClure Phillips.
1934   *Ethics: Origin and Development*. New York: Dial.
1968a   "Modern Science and Anarchism." Pp. 146-94 in Roger N. Baldwin, ed., *Kropotkin's Revolutionary Pamphlets*. New York: Benjamin Blom.
1968b   "Prisons and Their Moral Influence on Prisoners." Pp. 220-35 in Roger N. Baldwin, ed., *Kropotkin's Revolutionary Pamphlets*. New York: Benjamin Blom.
Lasch, Christopher
1979   *The Culture of Narcissism*. New York: Norton.
LeGuin, Ursula
1975   *The Dispossessed*. New York: Avon.
Lipton, Douglas, Robert Martinson, Judith Wilkes
1975   *The Effectiveness of Correctional Treatment*. New York: Praeger.
Mankoff, Milton
1978   "On the Responsibility of Marxist Criminologists: A Reply to Quinney." *Contemporary Crises* 2 (July): 293-301.
Martinson, Robert
1974   " 'What Works?' Questions and Answers about Prison Reform." *The Public Interest* (spring), pp. 22-54.
Maslow, Abraham
1969   *Psychology of Science: A Reconnaissance*. Chicago: Regnery.
Mattick, Hans
1973   " 'The Pessimistic Hypothesis' and 'An Immodest Proposal.' " *Public Welfare* 31 (spring) : 2-5.
May, Rollo
1969   *Love and Will*. New York: Norton.
McAnany, P., D. Sullivan, E. Tromanhauser
1973   "The Ex-Offender Movement in Chicago: Preliminary Observation of a Pilot Study." Paper presented at the annual meeting of the American Society of Criminology, Toronto, Canada.
Miller, David
1976   *Social Justice*. Oxford: Clarendon.
Miller, Martin
1973   "To Keep until Cured." Berkeley: University of California, unpublished paper.
Miller, William
1974   *A Harsh and Dreadful Love*. New York: Image.
Mitford, Jessica
1973   *Kind and Usual Punishment: The Prison Business*. New York: Knopf.
Moore, Barrington, Jr.
1972   *Reflections on the Causes of Human Misery and upon Certain Proposals to Eliminate Them*. Boston: Beacon.
Moran, Gabriel
1972   *The Present Revelation*. New York: Herder and Herder

Moynihan, Daniel
    1969   *Maximum Feasible Misunderstanding*. New York: Free Press.
Mumford, Lewis
    1967   *Technics and Human Development*. New York: Harcourt Brace
           Jovanovich.
    1970   *The Pentagon of Power*. New York: Harcourt Brace
           Jovanovich.
Nagel, William C.
    1973   *The New Red Barn: A Critical Look at the Modern American Prison*.
           New York: Walker.
National Criminal Justice Information and Statistics Service *Trends in Expenditures*
    1976   *and Employment Data for the Criminal Justice System: 1971-1974*.
           Washington, D.C.; U.S. Government Printing Office.
Newman, Graeme
    1978   *The Punishment Response*. Philadelphia: Lippincott.
Nouwen, Henri
    1975   *Reaching Out: The Three Movements of the Spiritual Life*. New York:
           Doubleday.
O'Connor, James
    1973   *The Fiscal Crisis of the State*. New York: St. Martin's.
Ohlin, Lloyd E., Robert B. Coates, and Alden D. Miller
    1974   "Radical Correctional Reform: A Case Study of the Massachusetts Youth
           Correctional System." *Howard Educational Review* 44 (February):
           74-111.
O'Leary, Vincent
    1974   "Parole Administration." Pp. 909-48 in Daniel Glaser, ed., *Handbook
           of Criminology*. Chicago: Rand McNally.
O'Leary, Vincent, and David Duffee
    1971   "Correctional Policy: A Classification of Goals Designed for Change."
           Crime and Delinquency 17 (October): 342-86.
Olson, Charles
    1969   *Causal Mythology*. San Francisco: Four Seasons.
    1970   *A Special View of History*. Berkeley: Oyez.
Palmer, Ted
    1975   "Martinson Revisited." *Journal of Research in Crime and Delinquency*
           12 (July): 133-52.
Pepinsky, Harold E.
    1976   *Crime and Conflict*. New York: Academic Press.
    1978   "Communist Anarchism As an Alternative to the Rule of Criminal
           Law." *Contemporary Crises* 2 (July): 315-34.
Piven, Frances Fox, and Richard Cloward
    1977   *Poor People's Movements: How They Succeed, How They Fail*.
           New York: Pantheon.
Platt, Tony, and Paul Takagi
    1977   "Intellectuals for Law and Order: A Critique of the New 'Realists.'
           Crime and Social Justice 8 (fall-winter): 1-16.
Powelson, Harvey, and Reinhard Bendix
    1951   "Psychiatry in Prison." *Psychiatry* 14.
Proudhon, Pierre-Joseph
    1843   *De la création de l'ordre dans l'humanité, ou Principles d'organisation
           politique*. Paris.
    1858   *De la justice dans la revolution et dans l'eglise*. Paris.
    1888   *System of Economic Contradictions, or, the Philosophy of Poverty*.
           Boston: Benjamin Tucker.
    1970   "Du principe federatif," in Stewart Edwards, ed., *Selected Writings of
           Pierre-Joseph Proudhon*. London.

Quinney, Richard
1973   *The Critique of Legal Order: Crime and Control in Capitalist Society.* Boston: Little, Brown.
1974   *Criminal Justice in America: A Critical Understanding.* Boston: Little, Brown.
1977   *Class, State and Crime.* New York: McKay.
1978   "The Production of Marxist Criminology." *Contemporary Crises* 2 (July) : 277-92.
Rawls, John
1971   *A Theory of Justice.* Cambridge: Harvard University Press.
Reasons, Charles E., and Russell L. Kaplan
1975   "Tear Down the Walls? Some Functions of Prisons." *Crime and Delinquency* 21 (October) : 360-72.
Rogers, Carl R.
1961   *On Becoming a Person* Boston: Houghton Mifflin.
1977   *On Personal Power: Inner Strength and Its Revolutionary Impact.* New York: Delacorte.
Rothman, David
1971   *The Discovery of the Asylum.* Boston: Little, Brown.
Rusche, George and Kirchheimer, Otto
1968   *Punishment and Social Structure.* New York: Russell and Russell.
Sartre, Jean-Paul
1957   *Existentialism and Human Emotions.* New York: Philosophical Library.
Schrag, Clarence
1974   "Theoretical Foundations for a Social Science of Corrections." Pp. 705-43 in Daniel Glaser, ed., *Handbook of Criminology.* Chicago: Rand McNally.
Schumacher, E. F.
1975   *Small Is Beautiful: Economics As If People Mattered.* New York: Harper & Row.
Slater, Philip
1970   *The Pursuit of Loneliness.* Boston: Beacon.
Somodevilla, S. A.
1978   "The Psychologists Role in the Police Department." *Police Chief* (April).
Studt, Eliot, Sheldon Messinger, and Thomas Wilson
1968   *C-Unit: Search for Community in Prison.* New York: Russell Sage.
Sullivan, Dennis
1979   "Out from Beneath the Angry Winter: Mutual Aid As a Foundation for Justice As If People Mattered," paper presented at the annual meeting of the Society for the Study of Social Problems (August). Boston.
Sullivan, D., E. Elvin, T. Dexter
1977   "Probation As a Workplace: A Qualitative Analysis of the Job of a Probation Officer." New York State Division of Probation, Empire State Plaza, Albany.
Szasz, Thomas
1970   *The Manufacture of Madness: A Comparative Study of the Inquisition and the Mental Health Movement.* New York: Harper & Row.
Takagi, Paul
1975   "The Walnut Street Jail: A Reform to Centralize the Powers of the State." *Federal Probation* 39 (December) : 18-26.
Tifft, Larry
1978   "The Definition and the Evolution of Social Justice." Paper presented at the annual meeting of the American Society of Criminology (November). Dallas.
1979   "The Coming Redefinitions of Crime: An Anarchist Perspective." *Social Problems* 26 (April): 392-402.

Tifft, Larry, and Dennis Sullivan
 1977 "Anarchy: A Non-Sequitur of Criminology, A New Vision of Justice and Social Order without the State." Paper presented at the annual meeting of the American Society of Criminology (November). Atlanta.
 1979 *The Struggle to Be Human: Crime, Criminology and Anarchism.* Orkney Islands, Over-the-Water-Sanday: Cienfuegos Press.
Toffler, Alvin
 1970 *Future Shock.* New York: Random House.
Tolstoy, Leo
 1919 "Appeal to Social Reformers." Pp. 100–17 in Waldon R. Brown, ed., *Man or the State.* New York: Huebsch.
Treger, Harvey
 1975 *The Police: Social Work Team.* Springfield, Ill.: Charles C. Thomas.
Trungpa, Chogyam
 1976 *The Myth of Freedom.* Berkeley: Shambhala.
U.S. Bureau of the Census
 1974 *Statistical Abstract of the United States.* Washington, D.C.; U.S. Government Printing Office.
Van den Haag, Ernest
 1975 *Punishing Criminals.* New York: Basic Books.
Von Hirsch, Andrew
 1976 *Doing Justice: The Choice of Punishments.* Report of the Committee for the Study of Incarceration. New York: Hill & Wang.
Ward, Colvin
 1973 *Anarchy in Action.* New York: Harper & Row.
Watts, Alan
 1975 *Tao: The Watercourse Way.* New York: Pantheon.
Wieck, David
 1962 "The Habit of Direct Action." *Anarchy* 13.
Wilks, Judith, and Robert Martinson
 1976 "Is the Treatment of Criminal Offenders Really Necessary?" *Federal Probation* 40 (March): 3–9.
Wilson, Colin
 1956 *The Outsider.* Boston: Houghton Mifflin.
Wilson, Edward O.
 1978 *On Human Nature.* Cambridge: Harvard University Press.
Wines, E. C., and Theodore Dwight
 1867 *Report on the Prisons and Reformatories of the United States and Canada.* Albany, N.Y.
Wolfe, Tom
 1976 *Mauve Gloves and Madman, Clutter and Vine.* New York: Farrar, Straus & Giroux.
Woodcock, George
 1972 *Pierre-Joseph Proudhon: His Life and Work.* New York: Schocken.
Zablocki, Benjamin
 1971 *The Joyful Community.* Baltimore: Penguin.

ABOUT THE AUTHOR

Dennis Sullivan is the author of various articles and monographs on criminal justice. He and Larry Tifft are also the co-authors of *The Struggle To Be Human: Crime, Criminology and Anarchism* (1979).